PIRATES OF THE PACIFIC, 1575–1742

THOMAS CAVENDISH AND THE *Santa Cruz* OF GUATULCO
From a painting in the Cathedral of Oaxaca.

PIRATES
of the Pacific,
1575-1742

PETER GERHARD

University of Nebraska Press
Lincoln and London

First Bison Book printing: 1990

Library of Congress Cataloging-in-Publication Data
Gerhard, Peter, 1920–
[Pirates on the west coast of New Spain, 1575–1742]
Pirates of the Pacific, 1575–1742 / Peter Gerhard.—1st Bison book
print.
p. cm.
Reprint. Originally published: Pirates on the west coast of New Spain,
1575–1742. Glendale, Calif.: A. H. Clark Co., 1960.
Includes bibliographical references (p.   ).
ISBN 0-8032-7030-5
1. Mexico—History—Spanish colony, 1540–1810. 2. Pirates—
Mexico—Pacific Coast—History. 3. Buccaneers—History.
4. Pacific Coast (North America)—History. 5. Pacific Coast
(Central America)—History. I. Title.
F1231.G4   1990
972'.02—dc20
90-33807   CIP

Reprinted by arrangement with the Arthur H. Clark Company

Originally published as *Pirates on the West Coast of New Spain,
1575–1742*

Contents

Illustrations

Preface

Piracy in America had its origin in the commercial and political rivalry between Spain on one side and England and France on the other.[1] In the late fifteenth and early sixteenth centuries Spain had acquired a huge part of the American continent, and jealously tried to exclude all other nations from participating in the great flow of wealth from her American mines. This silver and gold, originating mostly in Peru (including what is now Bolivia) and to a lesser extent in Mexico, constituted almost a worldwide monopoly of precious metals and was in theory exchangeable only for Spanish merchandise.[2] At the same time, England and France were emerging as important manufacturing nations with a great hunger for markets. They were also developing fleets of merchant ships manned by crews who came to excel the Spaniards in seamanship.

---

[1] The subject of piracy in the Caribbean has been treated extensively by Haring, *Buccaneers in the West Indies;* Burney, *History of the Buccaneers;* Masefield, *Spanish Main;* Esquemeling, *Buccaneers of America;* and others. For a Spanish point of view, also see Zaragoza, *Piraterías de los ingleses.*

[2] Haring, *Spanish Empire in America,* 315, and Priestley, *José de Gálvez,* 23, point out that in fact a large part of the goods shipped in Spanish bottoms from Spain to America came originally from England, France, and other European countries.

Spain's rivals in commerce and empire at the outset attempted peaceful trade with the new Spanish colonies in the Caribbean, sending ships loaded with finished goods, clothing, household articles, and hundreds of readily salable items. The first such voyage appears to have been a French one, in 1506. England's initial effort at this trade was perhaps the voyage of John Rut, sent by Henry VIII to Santo Domingo in 1527. Spain was neither able nor willing to furnish her American colonists with sufficient goods, even at unreasonable prices. Consequently there was a demand for English and French products which resulted in a brisk contraband trade, at first tolerated and even encouraged by some Spanish officials. But the royal order against foreign interlopers in the Spanish Indies was increasingly and harshly enforced, and the peaceful English and French traders became aggressive, many of them turning into sea robbers and looters of Spanish ports and shipping. By 1540 piracy, with more or less open encouragement from the French and English governments, had become a thriving business in the Caribbean.[3]

When England turned Protestant an element of religious fanaticism was injected into her rivalry with Spain. Then in the 1560s Holland rebelled from Spanish rule, emerging as a strong, Protestant,

---

[3] By no means did all contraband traders become pirates. Illicit trade with the Spanish colonies became increasingly widespread and profitable in the 17th and 18th centuries, thriving on the Spanish commercial policy which deliberately starved the American markets in order to force up prices. Cf. Priestley, op. cit., 29.

commercial, seafaring nation intent on getting its share of world trade. Now Spain was confronted by three powerful enemies who, in spite of occasional periods of truce, harassed her treasure galleons and even attacked her islands and mainland possessions on the eastern side of America.

A distinction should be drawn between three types of aggression employed by Spain's rivals: contraband trade, piracy, and acts of war. Certainly there is a difference between the cutthroat François l'Ollonais and the gentle British admiral, George Anson. Eventually the time arrived when England, France, and Holland joined forces with Spain in suppressing independent piracy. But to the Spanish government with few exceptions *all* foreign intruders in America were pirates and were treated as such (very badly indeed) if captured. Conversely the result could be much the same to a Spanish colonial if he were taken by a man-of-war, a privateer, an armed smuggler, or a pirate. In each category there were extremes of cruelty and leniency, but the goal of all was Spanish treasure and the humbling of Spanish pride.

Among the Elizabethans, Oxenham and Drake probably should be considered pirates because England was not at war with Spain at the time of their raids in the Pacific. In the same strict sense Cavendish was a privateer indulging in legalized robbery, as was Richard Hawkins a few years later. That Spain sometimes recognized this difference is evident in her treatment of Oxenham and

Hawkins, both of whom were captured. The first
was executed (although charged with heresy, not
piracy), while the other eventually was released in
honor. Following the same legalistic definition
with the Dutch raiders, Speilbergen was a pirate
and Schapenham was not. The Caribbean buccaneers who invaded the South Sea were a different
sort altogether, really pirates, but even there a fine
distinction could be drawn. When Dampier sailed
in the Pacific in 1680 he was undoubtedly a pirate,
but piracy against Spain was then condoned and
even encouraged by England. By the time he made
his next voyage, in 1685, England had agreed to
suppress piracy and Dampier was an outlaw. On
his third Pacific incursion in 1704 he was a legal
privateer, England being at war with Spain. Yet
there was no particular difference in the motives of
the three expeditions, nor in the men who sailed on
them, nor in their treatment of the Spaniards. Any
attempt to classify too strictly in this matter is apt
to become a splitting of hairs.

As has been suggested, the lot of a foreign ship
in Spanish Caribbean waters was by no means a
carefree one. Spain's reaction to interlopers was
both defensive and aggressive. The fleet, or convoy
system, was adopted for the clumsy treasure galleons, and fortifications were built to protect certain ports. Later the *Armada de Barlovento* was
organized, under the command of the viceroy of
New Spain, in an effort to rid the Caribbean of
pirates once for all. This fleet of warships not only

did convoy service but also pursued pirates and occasionally captured them. In the latter case prisoners were sometimes put to death or turned over to the Inquisition, but more often ended their lives as slaves. However, the Caribbean, with islands in the hands of the English, French, and Dutch, had numerous safe harbors where pirates and privateers could escape their pursuers, spend their hard-earned booty in wild sprees, and replenish their stores for another foray. All the wealth bound from America to Spain had to cross these waters in extremely unwieldy ships, some of which became easy prey to the waiting sea dogs. The many undefended Spanish settlements along and near the coast were another attraction which yielded a certain amount of loot. The Caribbean, in fact, offered so many incentives to pirates that it became overrun with them. Competition became such a problem that inevitably some of these sea rovers were drawn to the Pacific, or South Sea.

To the pirate or privateer the Pacific side of Spanish America had both advantages and serious drawbacks. The Spaniards, feeling secure in their private sea, at first found no need for protection from foreign enemies. Even after intruders appeared the king was reluctant to spend money on fortifying his ports in the South Sea. North of Panamá the only place with any real defense was Acapulco, and even there a castle was not built until forty years after the first foreign incursion into the Pacific. Nor was there, at first, any regular

Spanish fleet of warships for defending Pacific ports and shipping. Only in emergencies were the viceroys of Peru and New Spain able to conscript private vessels and arm them for defense purposes.[4] There were rich prizes to be taken – the silver ships running from Peru to Panamá and Mexico, and the fabulous Manila galleons – and they were often without means of repelling an attack. Even in the matter of small arms, so important in boarding and close fighting, the pirates always seemed to have the advantage. Often the Spaniards had only lances, or at best old harquebuses and flintlocks, while the enemy usually had the latest type muskets.

However, the difficulties of carrying out a piratical excursion in the Pacific were sometimes overwhelming. First it was necessary either to cross the jungles of Central America and hope to seize a Spanish ship in the Pacific, or to make the long and dangerous trip through the Straits of Magellan or around Cape Horn, a voyage often lasting a year or more. Once in the South Sea the intruders had no friendly ports of refuge, as in the Caribbean, but must take their chance on finding some deserted cove or island for careening and watering. If they were lucky enough to acquire booty, there was no way for them to enjoy their wealth without making the equally tedious and hazardous voyage back to the Caribbean or on to

---

[4] After Drake's incursion a defense fleet of sorts was created exclusively to convoy the periodic silver shipments from Peru to Panamá.

Europe. Most of the Spanish wealth was in silver, often a nuisance because of its weight and quite impracticable to carry overland across the isthmus. Perhaps the greatest difficulty of all was the basic one of getting provisions. The pirates were obliged to spend an amazingly large part of the time foraging on a hostile coast where there were few farms and the cattle had been driven inland in anticipation of their coming. Often they were forced to the extremity of exchanging prisoners for food rather than money. If captured, their lot was apt to be even more unhappy than in the Caribbean. In short, piracy in the Pacific was an enterprise to be undertaken only by the hardiest. For a century only squadrons of war or semi-official expeditions with large financial support were able to invade the South Sea, and at no time were pirates on the west coast anywhere near as numerous as in the Caribbean. Of those who made the attempt some few were fabulously successful, but more returned empty-handed, and many did not return at all.

From the Spanish records we get a point of view sharply contrasting with the English and other sources, that of the often defenseless Spanish and mestizo sailors and settlers who came between the pirates and their booty. To the inhabitant of the west coast of New Spain piracy was a scourge which affected him in a very personal way, and he could scarcely be blamed for looking on the pirates as unprincipled thieves and scoundrels to be dealt with harshly when the opportunity was presented.

This study is confined to piratical and other foreign incursions on the Pacific coast from Panamá north, beginning in 1575 or 1576 and continuing for the next 167 years. Often these expeditions had chroniclers aboard who kept records of their cruises, many of which were published. In the Spanish colonial archives there is much additional information, including accounts of some intruders and pirate bands of which we have no other record. Only a brief outline is given here of the pirates' movements and activities within the geographical limits described. Additional details may usually be found in the sources cited. All dates after 1582 are given according to the Gregorian calendar, or New Style. A number of the terms used here which may be unfamiliar to the reader, or which are used in a special sense, are explained in a glossary following the text.

The author wishes to thank those who have helped him in his research for this work. He is especially indebted to the directors and staffs of Archivo General de Indias, Sevilla; Bancroft Library at the University of California, Berkeley; Newberry Library, Chicago; and the Library of Congress, Washington. Dr. John W. Caughey kindly gave his permission to use an article from *Pacific Historical Review,* which appears here, in part, as the latter portion of Chapter IV.

I
The West Coast of New Spain

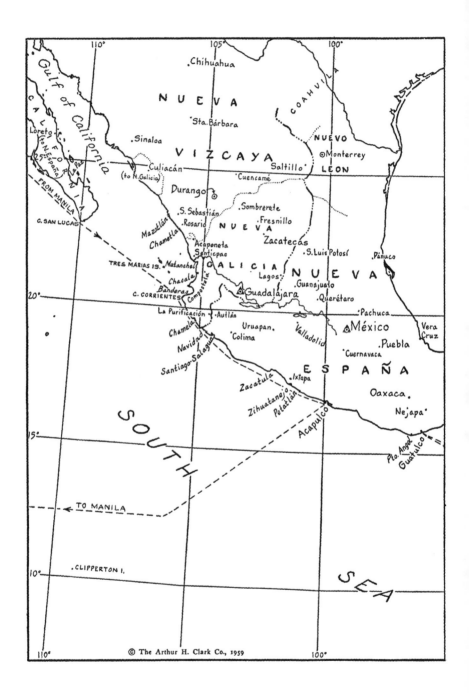

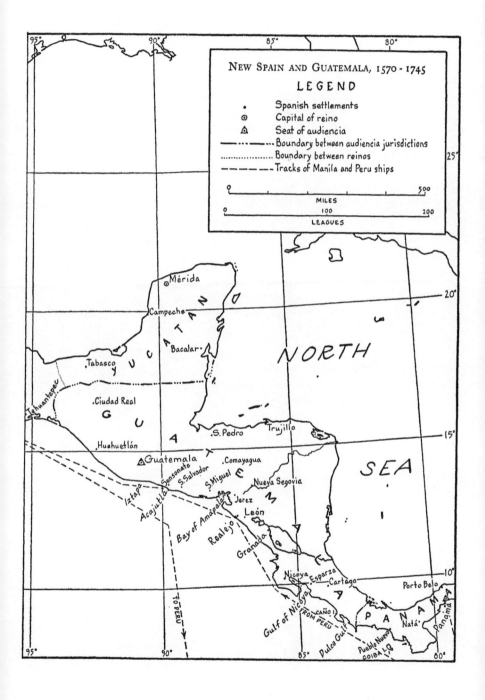

NEW SPAIN AND GUATEMALA, 1570 - 1745

LEGEND

.   Spanish settlements
⊙   Capital of reino
△   Seat of audiencia
—·—·— Boundary between audiencia jurisdictions
·············· Boundary between reinos
— — — — Tracks of Manila and Peru ships

MILES
0   500

0   100   200
LEAGUES

⊙Mérida

Campeche

Bacalar.

.Tabasco

NORTH

Tehuantepec

.Ciudad Real

G

Huehuetlán

.S. Pedro   Trujillo

A

△Guatemala   .Comayagua

Sonsonate   .S. Salvador

Iztapa   Acajutla   S. Miguel

.Jerez

León

Bay of Amapala

Realejo

Granada

Nueva Segovia

E

M

A

SEA

Nicoya   Esparza

.Cartago

Porto Belo

Gulf of Nicoya

CAÑO I.

FROM PERU

TO PERU

A

Natá.

P A N A M

Panama

Dulce Gulf

Pueblo Nuevo

COIBA I.

The West Coast of New Spain
1570-1750

From the "discovery" of the Pacific by Núñez de Balboa in 1513, the Spanish conquest and occupation of its shore proceeded quite rapidly until, by 1550, nearly all the coastal Indians from Panamá to about 22° N. had been subdued. There was a rather dense Indian population along most of this coastal area, but it was very much reduced by disease and other factors within five to twenty-five years after the arrival of the Spaniards.[1] Spanish settlements were few, partly because of the early extermination of Indian laborers, although in any case the more temperate highlands were preferred for colonization. After 1550 the conquest continued northward more slowly, reaching the valley of the Sinaloa by the end of that century and the Yaqui River toward the middle of the next. By 1700 Jesuit missionaries were in control of the coast of Sonora north to the vicinity of Guaymas and had begun subduing the primitive Indians across the gulf. The reduction of Lower California spread in both directions from Loreto, reaching the south-

---

[1] Sauer, *Colima of New Spain*, 93. Paso y Troncoso, *Papeles de Nueva España, 2a serie*, IV, pp. 236, 239-240, 249-250, 291. Letter from viceroy, February 7, 1554, in *México* 19, AGI.

ern tip of the peninsula in 1730, while Upper California was not settled until after 1769.

POLITICAL DIVISIONS

VICEROYALTY OF PERU.

The Isthmus of Panamá was, for most of the period with which we are concerned, attached to the viceroyalty of Peru, but a separate *audiencia* and bishop had their headquarters at Panamá City. The jurisdiction of the *audiencia* of Panamá extended through the province of Veragua (now the western part of the Republic of Panamá) to Burica Point, where it met the *audiencia* and captaincy general of Guatemala.

GUATEMALA

From Burica Point north and west almost to Tehuantepec extended the captaincy general and *audiencia* of Guatemala. While the viceroy of New Spain in theory had certain jurisdiction over this territory, in fact it was quite independent of him. The *capitán general* residing in Santiago de Guatemala (now Antigua) was also president of the *audiencia,* and reported directly to the king. Subordinate to him and ruled by *gobernadores* and *alcaldes mayores* were a number of vaguely defined provinces. On the west coast these included, from south to north, Costa Rica, Nicoya, Nicaragua, San Miguel, San Salvador, Sonsonate, Guatemala, and Soconusco.

VICEROYALTY OF NUEVA ESPANA (NEW SPAIN)

Beginning with the province of Tehuantepec, the territory subordinate to the viceroy of Nueva España stretched west and north to California and beyond. The viceroy had his court in the city of Mexico and was responsible in a military sense for a vast region extending from the West Indies to the Philippine Islands.[2] He was also president of the *audiencia* of Mexico, whose jurisdiction included the peninsula of Yucatán. There was a separate and independent *audiencia* at Guadalajara with judicial (and to a large extent political) control over the kingdoms of Nueva Galicia and Nueva Vizcaya, including the coast north of Navidad Bay. The Californias were directly under the viceroyalty of Nueva España. Along the coast, local government was entrusted to *alcaldes mayores* in the few Spanish settlements. These were, more than mayors, actually governors of often considerable territories, and exercised extensive powers within their jurisdictions. The coastal *alcaldías mayores* in Nueva España proper were Tehuantepec, Guatulco, Acapulco, Zacatula, Colima, and Autlán. Those in the *audiencia* of Guadalajara were La Purificación, Compostela, San Sebastián, and Culiacán.

---

[2] Letter from viceroy, November 27, 1710, in *México* 485, AGI.

PORTS AND TOWNS NEAR THE COAST

The first Spanish settlements on the Pacific were in the Isthmus of Panamá. The village of Natá was settled in 1517. Two years later the city of Panamá was founded six miles northeast of its final site. It was a swampy, ill-chosen location with little in its favor but strategic importance. Panamá was the terminus of the treasure ships which brought silver and gold from Peru, to be carried across the isthmus and transshipped to Spain. It was also the depot for all Spanish goods destined for South America. The *audiencia* was responsible for receiving the Peruvian bullion and seeing that it got safely across the isthmus. Because of the extreme tidal range, ships had to anchor some three leagues (seven miles) southwest of the old city, at Perico Point. The original Panamá was mostly of wooden construction, and when visited by Gage in 1637 had a fort (Fuerte de la Natividad) and a few pieces of cannon on the seaward side but was undefended from the land.[3] It was taken (from the land side), looted, and burned by Morgan in 1671, after which a new city was erected on the present site. In new Panamá extensive fortifications were built, including a stone wall completely surrounding the city with sufficient cannon to discourage any further attack.[4] Again most of the houses were

---

[3] Gage, *Travels,* 327. See also the description of the city and fortifications in 1640, in *Colección de libros y documentos,* 37.

[4] Dampier, *New Voyage,* 127.

of wood and were destroyed by fire in 1737, after which more stone and brick were used in construction.

Along and near the coast west of Panamá were a number of small Spanish settlements (Natá, Villa de los Santos, Pueblo Nuevo, Santiago Alanje or Chiriquí), but much of the country was deserted. The inhabitants lived from cattle raising, lumbering, subsistence agriculture, and gold mining.[5]

A convenient hide-out used many times by pirates was Coiba, or Quibo, a wooded, mountainous island twenty-two miles long and twelve miles from the mainland. Coiba had no permanent inhabitants, although occasionally pearl divers and fishermen camped on its shores. There was plenty of water and small game.

Between the provinces of Veragua and Costa Rica was a wild, mountainous country inhabited by Indians whom the Spaniards never completely subdued. Dulce Gulf, a large, deep, well-protected bay, had no Spanish settlement nearby and was consequently used by pirates as a port of refuge and a careening and watering place. Another such hide-out was Caño Island, off San Pedro Point, which also had fresh water.

In the latitude of 10° N. is the spacious and protected Gulf of Nicoya, also known in colonial times

---

[5] Peralta, *Costa-Rica Nicaragua y Panamá*, 172-174, 527-535. Vázquez de Espinosa, *Compendio*, 288-289.

as Salinas Gulf. Its shores were colonized at an early date, there being two principal Spanish-mulatto settlements. One, called Nicoya, was near the mouth of the Tempisque River at the head of the gulf, with a shipyard and of sufficient importance to have an *alcalde mayor* much of the time. The other was at the Bay of Caldera, near the mouth of the gulf on the east shore, twenty leagues (sixty miles) from the capital of Costa Rica, Cartago. At Caldera there were several warehouses for the Panamanian and Peruvian trade, and a short distance inland was the Spanish village of Esparza (modern Esparta). In addition there were Christianized Indian villages on the west shore of the gulf and on Chira Island. Within the gulf were a number of unfrequented islands and coves occasionally used by pirates for careening and watering. The inhabitants of Nicoya province lived from agriculture and stock raising, their produce going to Panamá and Nicaragua.[6]

Not far above the Gulf of Nicoya is a deep, sheltered cove, Culebra Bay, described by the coast pilot as "the finest harbor in Central America."[7] Although quite close to the main colonial trail, it does not seem to have been used a great deal either by Spaniards or pirates. There were a few cattle ranches nearby when buccaneers called at Culebra in 1685-86.

---

[6] Vázquez de Espinosa, *op. cit.*, 242-244.
[7] Hydrographic Office, *Sailing Directions,* 207.

What is now the port of Corinto, in Nicaragua, was known until the late nineteenth century as Puerto de la Posesión or, more commonly, Realejo. It was the most important place on the coast of Central America. In early years the vicinity of the harbor itself was uninhabited except for a sentinel, the old town of Realejo being two leagues inland on a small river. It was connected by road with the city of León, colonial capital of Nicaragua, the final (after 1610) site of which was eight leagues to the east. Realejo began to be used as a shipyard and port for the Peruvian trade about 1530. The harbor is completely sheltered by a long island. The docks for launching ships were on the river's bank at the edge of the town, although normally ships did not go up that far. By the middle of the sixteenth century there was a sizable colony of European and mestizo carpenters, caulkers, sailmakers, and other specialists. Until 1585 the Manila galleons were built there.[8] After Drake passed by, breastworks were erected near the entrance to the creek running up to Realejo town, and these fortifications continued to be used during successive visits of pirates. A chain or boom of trees was sometimes placed across the river opposite the breastworks.[9]

Thirty leagues southeast of Realejo, beyond León, was the important colonial city of Granada.

---

[8] *México* 20, AGI.

[9] Peralta, *Costa-Rica Nicaragua y Panamá,* 572.

Although close to the Pacific, it had direct maritime communication with Porto Belo and Cartagena by way of Lake Nicaragua and the Desaguadero (San Juan River). Because of its relative wealth and its accessibility from both seas, Granada was attacked several times by pirates. Livestock and agricultural products were shipped from Nicaragua, both to Peru (via Realejo) and to Cartagena (via Granada and the Desaguadero). Other important articles of colonial trade were cotton cloth, pitch, and rigging.[10]

In the mountains northeast of Realejo was the gold mining town of Nueva Segovia (modern Ocotal), on the upper waters of the Segovia or Coco River. This was the northernmost town in colonial Nicaragua, and the source of pitch, or pine tar, for the shipyard of Realejo and for export to Peru.[11]

The next harbor, within the colonial province of Guatemala, was the Bay of Amapala, or Gulf of Fonseca. Inside the bay the chief anchorage used by the Spaniards was the port of Martín López, near the present site of La Unión and not far from the old town of San Miguel. The only other Spanish town near the shores of the bay was Jerez de Choluteca, on the east side. The islands of Meanguera and Amapala had Christianized Indian villages. Spanish ships not infrequently entered the

---

10 Vázquez de Espinosa, *op. cit.,* 230 ff.
11 *Ibid.,* 228.

bay to load pitch, cacao, and other products for Peru and Mexico. There was a regular ferry service from Martín López across to what is now Puerto Morazán in Nicaragua, to avoid the long mule trek around the swampy shores.[12] In spite of this lack of privacy, Amapala was used by foreign ships as a center of operations from 1684 to 1721.

The next colonial seaport, and a very important one despite its disadvantages, was the open roadstead of Acajutla. A shipyard was established there in the early 1530s but was soon abandoned in favor of Realejo. Then Acajutla became the shipping point for cacao (chocolate) grown in the vicinity, and was frequently called at by ships engaged in the trade between Mexico and Peru. It was the chief Pacific port for the entire province of Guatemala, which included what is now El Salvador. Nearby was the Spanish town of La Santísima Trinidad de Sonsonate, and somewhat farther were the cities of Santa Ana and San Salvador. Besides the principal crop of cacao, there was a good deal of subsistence agriculture and cattle raising in the surrounding country.[13]

The coast between Amapala and Guatulco was devoid of sheltered anchorages, but there were a few Spanish towns near the sea, including Chiquimula, Huehuetlán, and Tehuantepec.

12 *Ibid.*, 216. Gage, *Travels,* 306.

13 Vázquez de Espinosa, *op. cit.,* 210. Paso y Troncoso, *Epistolario,* IX, p. 149. According to a document of 1562 in the latter, 50,000 *cargas* of cacao were shipped yearly from Acajutla to Mexico.

Guatulco, or Huatulco, was the first seaport to be developed and used to any great extent by the Spaniards on the Mexican Pacific coast. It is a snug, sheltered bay well suited to the type of vessel in use during the colonial period, and the best natural harbor between Amapala and Acapulco, a distance of nine hundred miles.[14] It had fresh water, firm anchorage, and a smooth, sloping sandy beach for boat landing. A trail ran from Guatulco across the mountains to the important city of Oaxaca, forty-five leagues (c. 125 miles) inland, where it joined the main road to Mexico City. Three leagues from the sea to the northwest was the Indian village of Santa María Guatulco, from which the port took its name.[15]

The harbor of Guatulco came into use before that of Acapulco in spite of its much greater distance from the capital, because it was simpler to improve the existing Indian trail from Oaxaca than to open an entirely new road through the very rugged country between Cuernavaca and Acapulco.[16] Thus Guatulco became at an early date

---

[14] Hydrographic Office, *Sailing Directions*, 168. The H. O. chart still shows the old name "Port of Huatulco," although that bay is called Bahía de Santa Cruz by the present inhabitants. The adjacent bay to the east, called "Santa Cruz" on the chart, is now known as Bahía Chagüey.

[15] Santa María Guatulco was moved still farther inland to its present site (7 leagues, or c. 18 miles from the port) in the 18th century.

[16] Borah, *Colonial Trade*, 24. An excellent and well-documented study.

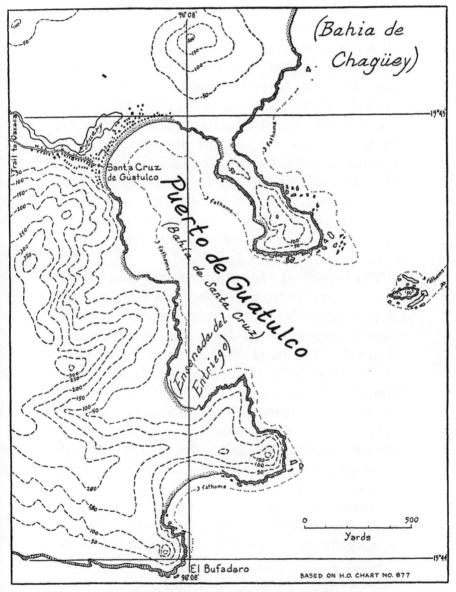

(Bahia de Chagüey)

Trail to Oaxaca

Estuary

Santa Cruz de Guatulco

Puerto de Guatulco

(Bahía de Santa Cruz)

(Ensenada del Entriego)

fathoms

fathoms

El Bufadero

0   500
Yards

BASED ON H.O. CHART NO. 877

THE PORT OF GUATULCO, ABOUT 1580
Position of houses is approximate. Modern names are shown in parentheses.

the northern terminus of maritime traffic between
New Spain and Peru. It also had an active local
trade with Central America. Sometime between
1537 and 1540 Guatulco began to be settled by
Spanish shipbuilders, business agents, storekeep-
ers, and government officials. A good number of
Indian laborers were moved down to the port.
Complete facilities and materials were assembled
there for building and refitting ships. By 1542 the
settlement was important enough to have a *corregidor* (later, *alcalde mayor*). It had a church, a
large customhouse, warehouses, and several hundred brush and wattle huts.[17]

The heyday of Guatulco was the period from
1540 to 1575. There were commonly three or four
ships a year to Peru, and a greater number of small
vessels engaged in the local trade with Central
America.[18] The latter consisted largely of the exchange of goods (clothing, livestock, Negro slaves)
from New Spain for cacao shipped from Acajutla.
Ships leaving Guatulco for Peru carried a varying
cargo of Mexican products and returned with
Peru's exports, silver and mercury. The value of
shipments from Guatulco was estimated in 1562
at 400,000 pesos annually.[19]

Guatulco's importance declined from about
1574, after Acapulco became the chief port of the
viceroyalty on the South Sea. The latter place was

---

[17] Pretty, *Voyage of Thomas Candish,* 814.
[18] Borah, *op. cit., passim.*
[19] Paso y Troncoso, *Epistolario,* IX, p. 149.

definitely established as the terminus for trans-Pacific trade with the Orient, and as the trans-shipment point for the extremely profitable extension of that trade to Peru. Guatulco continued for a time to handle a much diminished part of the local traffic with Peru and Central America, but by 1586 customs receipts at that port had dropped to less than 1,000 pesos a year.[20] Both Drake (1579) and Cavendish (1587) entered and rummaged Guatulco, sailing away with everything of value they could steal. Cavendish left the town in ashes. Such attacks were made easy by the fact that Guatulco had no fort, nor any defense whatever except the few Spaniards who might happen to be there. Perhaps to eliminate such a temptation to pirates, the viceroy in 1616 ordered that the village at Guatulco port be destroyed, the houses torn down, and the Indian population moved inland to Santa María.[21] Presumably from that date Guatulco ceased to be a legal port of exit and entry.

While there is some evidence that Guatulco was used for contraband shipment of Chinese goods to Peru after 1616,[22] as far as we know the port remained deserted except perhaps for a sentinel and an occasional fisherman or local coasting boat from Central America. Several pirates called there to take shelter and fill their water casks, or rummage the surrounding country for provisions.

[20] Letter from viceroy, February 23, 1586, in *México* 20, AGI.
[21] Letter from viceroy, May 25, 1616, in *México* 28, AGI.
[22] *México* 29, AGI.

When the English captains Swan and Townley went in there in 1685 they found the port abandoned and no trace of the former town except "a little chapel standing among the Trees, about 200 paces from the Sea." [23]

Puerto de los Angeles, or Puerto Angel, just west of Guatulco, was not used by the Spaniards to any extent, but it was occasionally called at by pirates.

Acapulco, Mexico's only developed seaport on the Pacific for much of the colonial period, was discovered by the Spaniards in 1521 and was probably first settled about 1530.[24] It has a fine sheltered harbor of easy access, by far the best and most spacious on the Mexican coast south of Lower California. An additional advantage is its relative closeness (110 leagues, or 280 miles) to the city of Mexico.

However, the extremely rugged nature of the country between Mexico City and Acapulco constituted a serious communications problem in the sixteenth century. There was a good trail south to Cuernavaca, but beyond there the mountains and innumerable river crossings made travel by horse or mule impossible. The trip took about a month on foot, and everything had to be carried on the

---

[23] Dampier, *New Voyage*, 164. In 1959 the bay had a single fisherman's family.

[24] According to Wagner, *Cartography of the Northwest Coast*, I, p. 14, Acapulco was settled about 1530. There was probably a shipyard there even before that. Orozco y Berra, *Apéndice al Diccionario Universal*, I, p. 29, says the settlement did not actually begin until 1550.

backs of Indian *tamemes*. Consequently, in the early years of Spanish occupation Acapulco was used only by an occasional exploring ship. All trade with Central America and Peru was at first handled through the more accessible port of Guatulco. It was not until the late 1560s that a fair trail was opened from Mexico City, and even then the numerous unbridged rivers made it preferable to continue using Guatulco.[25]

When the king ordered a trade route opened between New Spain and the Orient he entrusted the leadership of the expedition to a priest-navigator, Andrés de Urdaneta. Urdaneta sailed from the port of Navidad in November, 1564, crossed to the Philippines, and returned in October of the following year to Acapulco, which he recommended be made the terminus of trans-Pacific trade. Hordes of Indians were put to work making the trail from Mexico City passable to animals. When the first galleon arrived with Chinese merchandise, in 1573, an important bridge was still incomplete, making a long detour and dangerous ford necessary. The bridge seems to have been completed during the following year, reducing travel time almost by half.[26] The journey from

---

[25] Letter from viceroy, April 15, 1571, in *México* 19, AGI.

[26] *Ibid.* It is not clear which river was crossed by this important bridge. The two largest rivers on the trail, the Balsas and the Papagayo, had to be traversed on rafts in 1698 and 1804 (Gemelli Carreri, *Viaje a la Nueva España,* I, pp. 35, 38; Alessio Robles, *Acapulco,* 180). According to Alessio Robles, *op. cit.,* 177, the trail was made fit for mule travel by order of the viceroy D. Luis de Velasco in 1592.

Mexico to Acapulco could now be made in from six to ten days. The king's couriers, traveling day and night, customarily got through in three or four days. However the difficulty of transit continued to be a problem, and heavy objects such as cannon were usually sent around by way of the Isthmus of Tehuantepec. The trail was not made passable to wheeled vehicles until 1927.[27]

The Chinese trade had great repercussions on the economy of Spain and her American colonies. Luxury goods were much in demand in New Spain, and even higher prices could be obtained in Peru for the same merchandise. Each year for two and a half centuries the great unwieldy treasure galleons crossed and recrossed the Pacific, draining America of silver in exchange for silks, chinaware, beeswax, spices, perfumes, jewelry, and other fineries; and this in spite of many royal orders intended to limit and control the trade. Sometimes there were three or four ships crossing in the same year, but most of the time sailings were limited by law to two galleons, or a single galleon each year. Occasionally, owing to ship-wreck or the presence of an enemy, one or more years went by with no sailing at all. The value of the cargo usually varied from 200,000 to 1,000,000 pesos at Manila, worth two or three times that amount in New Spain and Peru. Contraband sometimes raised the final value to more than

---

[27] Alessio Robles, *op. cit.,* 185.

10,000,000 pesos. The westbound cargo was almost exclusively silver.[28]

With the opening of this tremendously profitable China trade, Acapulco became a lively place during the season when the galleons were in port. A sizable colony of craftsmen took up residence there: carpenters, caulkers, blacksmiths, and sailmakers. Warehouses were built to store supplies: rigging, the countless items needed to equip the galleons, and food which had to be brought from far in the interior.[29] For most of the year, because of its unhealthy situation and oppressive climate, Acapulco was deserted except for a small permanent population of Negroes, mulattoes, and Chinese (there were no Indians). It was a dirty, unattractive village, a hodgepodge of wood and mud huts with thatched roofs, hot and swarming with vermin and troublesome gnats, and a perfect breeding place for all sorts of tropical disease.[30]

The Manila galleons, as they were called by English writers (the Spaniards called them *naos de China*), generally arrived at Acapulco from late November to January, after a voyage from the Philippines lasting an average of five and a half months.[31] In the course of this long crossing

[28] An excellent study of the China trade is Schurz, *The Manila Galleon*.

[29] *México* 22, AGI.

[30] Gemelli Carreri, *op. cit.* I, pp. 22-26.

[31] The average length of thirty-seven recorded eastbound voyages between 1565 and 1758 was 170 days.

there were many deaths from scurvy, and those fortunate enough to reach Acapulco always arrived in an unhealthy and unwashed state which was only aggravated, after their arrival, by the insanitary condition of the place and the complete lack of comforts for travelers. As late as 1698 there was no hotel or inn at Acapulco.[32] The passengers arriving on the galleon, unless they chose to begin at once the rugged trip to Mexico City, had to compete with hundreds of merchants for accommodation in filthy shacks and convents. During the *feria* which followed the arrival of each galleon, usually in January or February, the town bulged with transients and the cost of living shot up – a situation that seems to have continued to the present time. A traveler in 1698 complained that "a man cannot eat well under one peso a day," an outrageous amount.[33]

Before the arriving galleon was unloaded, preparations were under way for the return voyage to Manila. Soldiers, convicts being deported to the Philippines, and passengers, came down from Mexico City; the ship was caulked and refitted, and supplies and silver were assembled for the westbound sailing. Under normal conditions this was shorter than the eastbound crossing, taking somewhat less than four months. The recommended time for leaving Acapulco was January

[32] Gemelli Carreri, *op. cit.,* I, p. 22.
[33] *Ibid.,* I, p. 24.

or February, since a later sailing meant probable contrary winds and arrival in the Philippines at the height of the typhoon season, but in spite of this danger departure was usually put off until the end of March or even April. Because of this delay more than one galleon was wrecked with the loss of everyone aboard.[34]

Supplementary to the Manila trade route was the extension of this traffic from Acapulco to Peru. Much higher prices were paid for Chinese merchandise in Lima than in Mexico. From the beginning the king and his councilors realized that such trade was eating into their share of Peruvian silver and violated the strict monopoly of the Spanish merchants. A series of royal orders prohibiting such traffic, either direct or by transshipment at Acapulco, reached America where they were skillfully evaded by everyone including the viceroys.[35] The ruling was half-heartedly enforced in 1589, after which date a thriving contraband trade was carried on by greasing the palms of the royal officials whose duty it was to prevent it. The Chinese goods were transferred from the Manila

---

[34] Of 148 recorded sailings from Acapulco between 1566 and 1784, two were in December, five in January, eleven in February, eighty-seven in March, forty-two in April, and one in May. This delay was caused intentionally by the Mexican merchants, who could get the Chinese goods at a lower price when they agreed among themselves not to buy until their Manila colleagues were anxious to begin the return voyage. The often fatal consequences of a late sailing were recognized by the viceroys, who ordinarily commanded the galleons to leave by a certain date.

[35] Borah, *Colonial Trade*, 119.

galleons to other ships waiting at Puerto Marqués, just across the bay, or even in the harbor of Acapulco itself, and thence transported to Peru. Another type of contraband, also prevalent, was the landing of undeclared goods at deserted ports before reaching Acapulco.

The China trade had been carried on for fifty years before any steps were taken to defend Acapulco against Spain's enemies. Drake, in 1579, did not attempt to visit the port, knowing that the Manila ship would have sailed at least a month before he could hope to arrive there. Cavendish, in 1587, coasted by within sight of the Paps of Acapulco, but also realized that the galleon's departure date had long since passed and that he would find little of value in the town. At the time of Cavendish's cruise the viceroy wrote, "Your majesty has not a single piece of artillery [on the entire coast]."[36] Nothing had been done toward fortifying Acapulco because of the expense involved.

When news of the Dutch pirate Speilbergen's imminent arrival reached Mexico in late 1614, there was a feverish attempt to improvise some kind of fort to protect Acapulco.[37] Soldiers and "volunteers" from all over the kingdom were rushed to the port to dig trenches and raise gun platforms on El Morro, the hill on the north side

[36] Letter from viceroy, October 30, 1587, in *México 21*, AGI.
[37] *Idem,* October 28, 1615, in *México 28*, AGI.

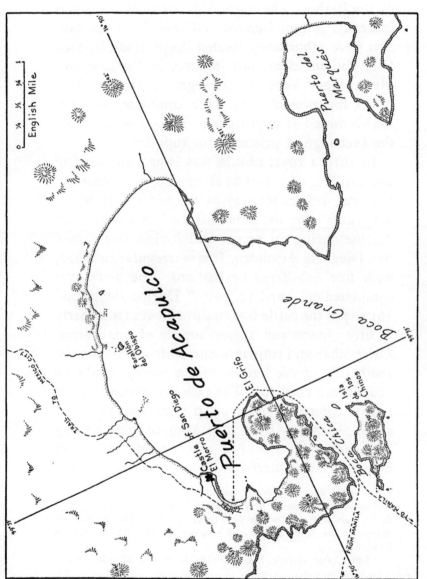

THE PORT OF ACAPULCO, ABOUT 1625

of the harbor. The normal garrison of forty was
increased to four hundred soldiers. Fourteen cannon were laboriously hauled down from Mexico
City and installed, just in time, in the new emplacements.[38] When Speilbergen sailed into Acapulco the preparations were complete, and the
Dutch found it expedient to request a truce for
the exchange of prisoners for supplies.

In 1616 a royal cédula was issued authorizing
the building of a fort at Acapulco, and construction was well under way by the end of the year.[39]
The *castillo,* on the same hill used as a temporary
defense during the recent Dutch visit, was named
San Diego de Acapulco. It was irregular in shape,
with five *caballeros* or bastions. The work was
completed on April 15, 1617.[40] During the period
1617-1742 the castle was equipped with from thirty
to fifty cannon and a good supply of small arms.
Later other gun emplacements were erected on the
south side of the harbor so the enemy would be
caught in a cross fire. The new fort seems to have
had a deterrent effect on pirates and probably
saved Acapulco from a sacking in 1624 during
Schapenham's visit. No other pirate ships are
known to have entered Acapulco, although Town-

[38] Portillo, *Descubrimientos,* 222, 224, 454.

[39] Letter from viceroy, May 25, 1616, in *México* 28, AGI. *Cf.* Calderón, *Fortificaciones en Nueva España,* 226-230. The engineer in
charge of the fort's design and construction was Adrian Boot, a
Dutchman!

[40] Letter from viceroy, May 24, 1617, in *México* 28, AGI.

ley (1685) and Anson (1742) sent boats in to reconnoiter the harbor. Each found it desirable to wait for the Manila galleon in a less defended place. The original fort of San Diego was ruined in an earthquake in 1776, and a new castle was completed on the same site in 1783.[41]

As at Guatulco, it would seem that the few Spaniards resident at Acapulco, royal officials and craftsmen, retired to higher altitudes during most of the year and only lived at the port from November to April. The ranking official and representative of the king was the *Castellano en propiedad de la Real Fuerza*. He also had the title of *Teniente General de las Costas del Mar del Sur,* and was in charge of any Spanish naval units on the Pacific coast. The size of the permanent garrison varied from forty to a hundred men, with two or three officers. This force was increased to two hundred or more when the China ship was in port. In the early eighteenth century there was also a civilian militia composed of all able-bodied Negroes, mulattoes, and Chinese, divided along racial lines into three companies.[42]

Zihuatanejo (variant spellings: Sihuatanejo, Siguatanejo, Ciguatanexo, Seguatanejo; also known as Chequetán), a well-protected harbor west of Acapulco, was not greatly used by the Spaniards and had no permanent settlement dur-

[41] Alessio Robles, *op. cit.,* 170-172. Calderón, *Fortificaciones,* 244.
[42] Villaseñor, *Theatro Americano,* I, pp. 186-189.

ing colonial times. This made it an advantageous place for enemy ships to careen, take on wood and water, and lie in wait for the Manila galleon.[43]

The next port beyond was that of Zacatula, near the mouth of the Balsas or Mexcala River. A ship-yard was established there by Cortés in 1522, and a Spanish settlement grew up around it, but both were almost abandoned some few years later.[44] This place was a poor anchorage and was rarely called at. Between Zacatula and Colima was the province of Motines, a largely depopulated area after an early period (c. 1523-1535) of gold min-ing.

The twin ports of Santiago and Salagua are in the northern part of what is now the Bay of Man-zanillo. A settlement may have been founded at Salagua before 1527, and although it was soon abandoned the two spacious and well-protected harbors were used extensively by Spanish explor-ers and pearlers.[45] There was a brook of fresh water at the head of Salagua Bay. Trails extended to the cities of Guadalajara and Colima, and northwest to Port Navidad. Both harbors served occasionally as ports of refuge for the Manila galleons. About the middle of the seventeenth century Salagua be-came a regular port of call for these ships on their

---

[43] Funnell, *Voyage Round the World,* 78, mentions a settlement of forty houses at Zihuatanejo in 1704, but it had disappeared by the time of Anson's visit in 1742.

[44] Sauer, *Colima of New Spain,* 7-9. Portillo, *Descubrimientos,* 338.

[45] Wagner, *Cartography of the Northwest Coast,* I, p. 13.

eastbound voyage to Acapulco, although later Navidad (see below) seems to have been called at more frequently. The *alcalde mayor* of Colima kept a sentinel there, with supplies of fresh fruit for the scurvy-ridden invalids who came ashore for the first time in many months. Except for the lookout and an occasional fisherman, Salagua was uninhabited throughout the colonial period, but it was used to a certain extent for contraband traffic with the galleons. The modern port of Manzanillo was not developed until mid-nineteenth century. Colima was the center of a fairly important cacao-producing area.

The tiny but secure bay known as Puerto de la Navidad, in 19° 14′ N., was discovered by the Spaniards in 1523 and became an important base for expeditions to California and beyond.[46] A royal shipyard was established before 1550 at the mouth of a lagoon at the east end of the bay. The ships of Urdaneta's squadron, which sailed to the Philippines in 1564, were built there, and at one time it was considered making Navidad the eastern terminus of trans-Pacific trade, but Acapulco was chosen instead. However, Navidad continued to be used by explorers and pearlers going to California. From 1585 it was the supply base and southern limit of an important pearl fishing monopoly.[47] Navidad was the northernmost Pacific harbor in

[46] Sauer, *op. cit.*, 10. Lebrón de Quiñones, *Relación Breve*, 11, 20.
[47] Gerhard, "Pearl Diving," 240.

New Spain proper, the coast beyond coming under the jurisdiction of the *audiencia* of Guadalajara. Navidad's most important function was that of a harbor of refuge for the Manila galleons. These ships, from the mid-seventeenth to the late eighteenth century, nearly always put in briefly at either Salagua or Navidad, which were directly on their course to Acapulco. The usual time of arrival was November or December. It was the responsibility of the *alcalde mayor* of Autlán to maintain a lookout at Navidad to watch for pirates and notify the authorities of the galleon's arrival. The sick were allowed to go ashore, and the more serious invalids remained to recuperate and continue by land to Mexico City. One of the officers or passengers from the ship was designated *gentilhombre* (king's courier) and given relays of horses to carry the official dispatches from Navidad to the capital, a distance of 215 leagues. Like Salagua, Navidad was a landing point for contraband goods from the China ships.

The anchorage of Chamela, in 19° 32′ N., is protected from all but the rare southerly winds by a number of rocks and islands. It was the southernmost port in Nueva Galicia, and in colonial times had a small fishing village on its shore. Chamela was connected by trail with the old town of La Purificación, fourteen leagues inland.[48]

Just beyond Cape Corrientes, which was the

---

[48] Portillo, *op. cit.*, 339. Dampier, *New Voyage*, 179.

landfall of the China ships coming down from San
Lucas, is the great open bay of the Valley of Banderas (Val de Banderas). It has several fairly
protected anchorages and a river (Río del Valle in
colonial times, modern Río de Ameca) which was
used by the Spaniards as a watering place and a
haven for small ships. In the valley behind the bay
were a number of Spanish farms and cattle
ranches.[49]

The next port north was the tiny cove or *ensenada*
of Chacala. This bay, a small indentation in the
coast somewhat protected by steep hills, was used
to a certain extent during the colonial period by
explorers and pearlers. When Cavendish called
here in 1587 he found two inhabited shacks on the
beach.[50] Throughout much of the seventeenth century Chacala was a supply base for expeditions to
Lower California.[51] In 1668 there was a small garrison there, subordinate to the nearby Spanish
town of Compostela. After 1700 Chacala's place
as the chief supply port for California was taken
by Matanchel (see below). The countryside around
Chacala was thinly settled, the chief occupations
being small-scale agriculture and cattle raising,
with periodic surges of silver mining activity.

Ensenada de Santiago de Matanchel (now
called Matanchén) is an open bay, protected from

[49] Portillo, *op. cit.*, 340. Mota y Escobar, *Descripción*, 66.
[50] Pretty, *Voyage of Thomas Candish*, 815.
[51] *México* 24, AGI. Portillo, *op. cit.*, 340.

the prevailing northwest wind, just east of the more recently developed port of San Blas. It was sometimes used as a harbor of refuge by early explorers and pearlers, and for a time the Manila galleons called there for watering.[52] Throughout the first half of the eighteenth century Matanchel was the principal seaport of Nueva Galicia and the supply point for the Jesuit missions in Lower California. Once each year the mission boat crossed from Loreto to Matanchel and returned with supplies, mail, and missionaries.[53] The port was reached by trail (115 leagues) from Guadalajara. On the shore was a small settlement of government officials, pearlers, and stevedores, although the place was nearly deserted except during the stay of the California boat. In 1768 the visitor-general José de Gálvez ordered a new town and garrison established at San Blas, three miles west of Matanchel, and the latter place disappeared from the map.

Near the mouth of the largest river in central Mexico, Río Grande de Santiago, was the "port" of San Pedro. Its value as a shipping point was limited by the bar at the river's mouth, and by the clouds of insects which infested the surrounding woods, but San Pedro was used occasionally by pearlers and explorers going to Lower California.

---

[52] Mota y Escobar, *Descripción*, 82.
[53] Clavigero, *Lower California*, 215. *Guadalajara*, 71, 134, and 205, and *México* 482, AGI.

Nearby was the small town of Senticpac (variant spellings: Centicpac, Sentipac, Centiquipaque, Sentispac, etc.), settled by Spaniards in the 1530s, later abandoned, and repopulated by mid-seventeenth century.[54]

One of the first places developed and used by the Spaniards as a Pacific port was Chametla. The original settlement of that name, founded by Nuño de Guzmán in 1532, was probably on the right bank of the Baluarte River about five miles from its mouth.[55] Even in the dry season there was enough water to allow small ships to cross the bar and get up to Chametla. Cortés used this place as a supply port for his expedition to Lower California in 1535, after which it seems to have been abandoned. It was resettled by Spaniards under Francisco de Ibarra in 1564. Chametla was the home port of pearlers who frequented the gulf coast of Lower California in the late sixteenth and early seventeenth centuries. Swan found the site uninhabited in 1686, but the mouth of the river was still being used as a shipping point for the silver mining town of Rosario, fifteen miles inland.[56]

In spite of its natural advantages as an anchorage, San Juan de Mazatlán was little used by the Spaniards. Probably because they were closer to

[54] Mota y Escobar, *op. cit.,* 83. Portillo, *op. cit.,* 484-485.
[55] Kelly, *Excavations,* 4.
[56] Dampier, *New Voyage,* 185.

Mexico, Chametla and Matanchel were preferred as bases for pearling and northern exploration. There was no settlement at the port of Mazatlán until the late eighteenth century.[57] However there was a garrison at San Sebastián (now Concordia), twenty-six miles inland, founded in 1567, and another known as Presidio de Mazatlán not far from what is now Villa Unión.[58] For most of the colonial period a member of the latter garrison was stationed at the port of Mazatlán to watch for enemies and Spanish ships needing supplies.

The peninsula of Lower California, which had no permanent Spanish settlement until the end of the seventeenth century, terminates in a jagged headland called Cape San Lucas, behind which there is a fairly protected cove known as San Lucas Bay (San Bernabé, Cavendish's Aguada Segura). Before 1730, when a Jesuit mission was founded at nearby San José del Cabo, San Lucas was sometimes visited by explorers and pearling expeditions, and almost every year after 1565 it was sighted by the returning China ships. It was an excellent spot for pirates to wait for the galleons, with facilities for watering and careening, but often difficult to reach from the south because of contrary winds.[59]

---

[57] Letter from Gálvez to viceroy, Santa Ana, August 15, 1768, in *Guadalajara* 416, AGI.

[58] Olea, "Historia de Mazatlán." Mota y Escobar, *op. cit.*, 89.

[59] Letter from Gálvez to viceroy, Santa Ana, September 8, 1768, in *Guadalajara* 416, AGI.

Off the coast were a number of deserted islands, rarely visited by the Spaniards, some of which were used by pirates and privateers for careening and watering and as bases for raids on shipping and on mainland settlements. The Tres Marías group was called at by enemy ships from 1686 to 1721. We have already mentioned the importance of Coiba Island as a pirate base. South of Panamá, Taboga and the Pearl archipelago (although occupied by the Spaniards) were used for that purpose, as was Cocos Island, three hundred miles off the mainland of Costa Rica.

SHIPPING

From the above it can be seen that maritime commerce on the west coast of Mexico and Central America, from 1575 to 1745, was concentrated in two main trade routes: that between Acapulco and the Orient, and that between Mexico and Peru. In addition there was a certain amount of local trade between Mexico and Central America, and from Central America to Panamá and Peru and return. North of Guatulco there was very little local traffic except for pearlers and the annual supply boat from Matanchel to Loreto (after 1697). From the enemy's point of view the best prizes by far were the Manila galleons. The east-bound galleons were particularly vulnerable as they closely followed the shore from California to

Acapulco, but their cargo comprised largely merchandise, with little specie. The Manila-bound
ships, carrying huge quantities of silver coin,
headed straight out to sea from Acapulco and
turned westward in the latitude of 12° or 13° N.
Next in opportunity for plunder were the ships
taking Peruvian silver to Panamá, but these were
relatively well defended. Occasionally a valuable
prize could be found going from Peru to Central
America or Mexico with silver. Finally there was
a certain amount of pearling activity, and with
luck valuable pearls could be taken.

The strict order limiting and often prohibiting
trade between the Spanish colonies was not generally obeyed in the Pacific, but on the other hand
there was little incentive for local trade. With the
exception of Panamá and Acapulco, which were
to be well defended, there were few ports where
loot would repay a pirate the trouble of a visit.

II
Elizabethan Pirates

Elizabethan Pirates

To John Oxenham, or Oxnam, belongs the distinction of being the first foreign enemy to sail against the Spaniards in the Pacific. He came from a well-to-do Devonshire family, and commanded one of Francis Drake's ships on an expedition to the Caribbean in 1572-73. In July 1572 Drake raided Nombre de Dios, the original Caribbean terminus of the silver trail across the Isthmus of Panamá. Early the next year Drake returned and, accompanied by Oxenham, crossed the isthmus to within a league of the city of Panamá. They succeeded in capturing a mule train loaded with Peruvian silver, and it was on this occasion that both Drake and Oxenham acquired the ambition to cruise against Spain in the virgin South Sea. We know very little about Oxenham, but from the few available sources we can infer that he was a competent navigator with a good deal of imagination and courage, short-tempered, and considerably swayed by his emotions.

On his return to England from the Panamá raid, Oxenham fitted out a ship of about 140 tons and sailed from Plymouth sometime in 1575 with a

crew of seventy men and boys.[1] They arrived on
the north coast of Panamá probably in late 1575,
when Oxenham renewed his previous alliance with
the maroons *(cimarrones)*, runaway Negro slaves,
who lived in the jungle and carried on sporadic
warfare against the Spaniards. The ship was
beached and hidden among the mangroves, and
Oxenham and his men went with the maroons for
twelve leagues through the jungle and over the
mountains to the headwaters of a stream flowing
into the Gulf of San Miguel, on the Pacific. Here
they spent some weeks building a pinnace with a
forty-five-foot keel, armed with two small guns
which they had hauled across the divide. They
floated their little ship downstream and sailed out
on the South Sea until they reached the Pearl or
King's Islands, directly athwart the shipping lane
into Panamá from the south.

After lying in wait for ten days Oxenham captured his first prize, a small ship on her way from
Quito to Panamá with 60,000 pesos in gold and a
good supply of food. Six days later the pirates took
a second bark from Peru loaded with 100,000 pesos
in silver bars. The Spaniards were unarmed and,
we can imagine, astonished at the appearance of
an enemy. One of the prizes had a "table of massie
gold, with emralds", and aboard was a lady pas-

[1] Hakluyt, *Voyages* (1958), 140-144. Wagner, *Sir Francis Drake's
Voyage,* 318. [Hawkins], *Observations,* 235 ff. Masefield, *Spanish
Main,* 98 ff. Burney, *Chronological History,* I, p. 293 ff. For the date
of Oxenham's voyage, see footnote 4, below.

senger with whom, according to Sir Richard Hawkins, Oxenham promptly fell in love. Hawkins's version of the story makes much of this love affair, blaming it for all of Oxenham's subsequent troubles.[2]

After rummaging the pearlers' settlements among the islands and securing a few pearls Oxenham returned to the mainland, where he released his prizes and all his prisoners with the exception (according to Hawkins) of the Spanish lady, who preferred to stay with him. His clemency cost Oxenham the friendship of the maroons, to whom he had promised to turn over his Spanish prisoners, and had the further effect of allowing word of his presence to reach the authorities in Panamá.[3]

The president of the *audiencia* of Panamá fitted out four galiots with one hundred soldiers under the command of Juan de Ortega, who caught up with the enemy in the Gulf of San Miguel near the mouth of the same river they had come down.[4] It would seem that Oxenham not only had quarreled with the maroons but was at outs with his own men over the division of spoils, and the pirates were in

---

[2] Hawkins, *op. cit.*, 236. Charles Kingsley, in *Westward Ho!*, made a very romantic tale out of this Hawkins version.

[3] According to Burney (*op. cit.*, 297) and Masefield (*op. cit.*, 100) it was the Negro pearl divers robbed by Oxenham who got word to Panamá about the pirates.

[4] Madariaga, *Fall of the Spanish American Empire*, 167, says the Spaniards under *Pedro* de Ortega overtook the pirates "on Tuesday of Holy Week, 1577," the only exact date we have for the Oxenham expedition. However, Masefield (*op. cit.*, 105) gives evidence that this skirmish occurred perhaps a year earlier.

a state of discord and confusion when they should have been retreating across the isthmus. Several skirmishes occurred in which some half of the Englishmen were killed. The others, including Oxenham, fled inland leaving their treasure to be recovered by the Spaniards.

Meanwhile the authorities at Nombre de Dios had discovered Oxenham's ship hidden on the north coast, and soon all the pirates were killed except for Oxenham and a few others who were taken prisoners to Panamá. Some were condemned to death there, while Oxenham and three of his officers were taken to Lima and tried for heresy by the Inquisition. It appears that they were still alive in October, 1580, but were executed soon afterward.[5] The only survivors of the expedition were five grommets, or ship's boys, who were probably sold as slaves in Lima.

Francis Drake was born in Devonshire about 1543.[6] Without schooling, almost illiterate, he went to sea as a boy and accompanied his cousin, John

[5] Nuttall, *New Light on Drake,* 2-3. The officers were Tomás Xervel [Thomas Harvey?], ship's master; John Butler, pilot; and Butler's younger brother.

[6] A great deal of scholarship has been devoted to the study of documents pertaining to Drake's career, and particularly to his voyage of 1577-1580. The two published primary sources are: *The World Encompassed by Sir Francis Drake* . . . (London, 1628; reprinted by Hakluyt Society with notes by W. S. W. Vaux, London, 1854); and *The Famous Voyage of Sir Francis Drake* . . ., inserted in Hakluyt, *The Principal Navigations* . . . (London, 1589; also

Hawkins, on several trading voyages to America and elsewhere. At the age of about twenty-four he commanded his first ship on a cruise to the Gulf of Mexico, where he was almost captured by the Spaniards. By 1572, when he made a successful attack on the Isthmus of Panamá, Drake was perhaps the most skilled navigator of his day as well as a thoroughly competent naval tactician and an adroit leader of men. Most important, he had a flare for dramatic show and pageantry well calculated to impress the haughty foes of England. At the time he began his circumnavigation of the globe, the voyage which interests us here, he already had acquired a reputation as an invincible pirate which had spread throughout Spanish America. The mere rumor of his presence was often enough to demoralize the enemy.

Drake left England on December 13, 1577, with four small ships and a pinnace. There has been a certain amount of controversy as to the various motives of his expedition, and the extent to which it was sponsored by Queen Elizabeth and her

included in Vaux, *supra*). Vaux (266-267) also gives the narrative of Nuño da Silva. A number of Spanish documents from Central America concerning Drake's voyage are reprinted in Peralta, *Costa-Rica, Nicaragua y Panamá*, 569-590. The documents found in Peralta and others were translated by Nuttall, *New Light on Drake*. Admirable treatises, using the above and other mss. sources, are in Corbett, *Drake and the Tudor Navy*, I, pp. 216-294, and Wagner, *Sir Francis Drake's Voyage*. The reader interested in sources is referred to the last two volumes. Since the present writer has practically nothing to add to such thorough documentation, footnotes in this section are used only for the few exceptions and for extraneous comments.

court. Wagner implies that its chief aim was the opening of a spice trade between England and the Orient.[7] A secondary object may have been the discovery of the Straits of Anian, generally believed in those days to connect the Pacific with the Atlantic somewhere north of California. It is most unlikely that Drake had any plans or instructions for establishing English colonies, as has been alleged by some writers. It seems fairly clear that in Drake's mind the great impelling purpose of his voyage was to acquire loot at the expense of Spain, inflicting as much damage as possible on the totally undefended Pacific coast of Spanish America. Drake held some sort of commission from his queen, probably an ordinary one without specifically authorizing him to commit unprovoked hostilities against the Spaniards. He was backed financially by a company of adventurers in which Queen Elizabeth probably had no open interest, since no state of war existed between England and Spain, but she profited in both a political and a monetary sense from the results of the expedition.[8]

The original complement of Drake's squadron numbered 164 men and boys, including several young gentlemen of noble families. The crews were mostly English, but there were also a number of French, Scottish, Basque, Flemish, and other

[7] Wagner, *Sir Francis Drake's Voyage,* 225 (see footnote 6, above).

[8] According to Corbett, *op. cit.,* I, p. 217, the queen invested £1,000 in the voyage.

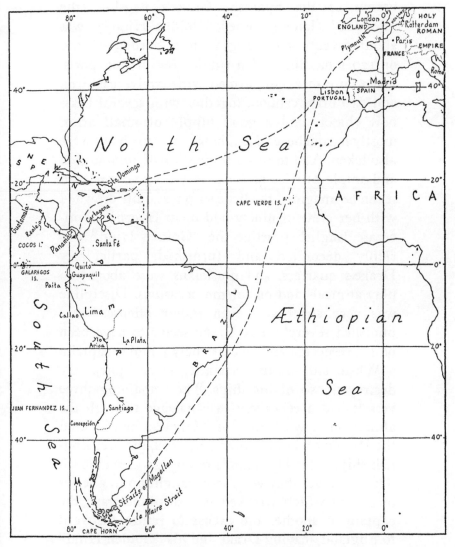

PIRATE ROUTES TO THE PACIFIC

sailors, as well as a few Negroes. Some of them had previously experienced service in the Pacific, in the vessels of the Spanish. Drake's flagship, the "Pelican" (later renamed "Golden Hind"), was about seventy feet long with a burden of 100 or 120 tons. She had a single row of gun ports, seven on either side, armed with twelve cast-iron and two brass cannon, together with several brass bow chasers and a good supply of small arms, mostly harquebuses. Longbows and crossbows were also taken. Add to this a large store of ammunition and ample provisions for a very long voyage, and it can be imagined the little ship was quite crowded with her crew of ninety-odd men. In order to increase English prestige the "Golden Hind" was richly decorated and furnished, particularly Drake's quarters, and musicians were aboard to play at meals and on solemn occasions. Discipline was very strict and even minor offenses were punished severely, but Drake seems to have been both a respected and an extremely popular captain.

While still in the Atlantic, Drake purposely destroyed two of his ships. The remaining three vessels had a relatively easy passage through the almost unknown Straits of Magellan and entered the Pacific early in September, 1578, the first English ships after Oxenham's to appear in the South Sea. However they were soon caught up in a series of storms which wrecked one ship and gave the captain of another the excuse to return eastward to England, leaving Drake and his "Golden Hind" to continue alone north along the coast of Chile. At Valparaíso Drake took his first Spanish prize and looted the tiny settlement, on December 5. He cruised northward, calling at most of the ports from Coquimbo to Callao, nearly everywhere taking the Spaniards by surprise and meeting with very little resistance. The richest ship seized was "Nuestra Señora de la Concepción," nicknamed "Cacafuego," captured off Ecuador on March 1, 1579, with a very large amount of silver and gold and sundry pearls and jewels.

The viceroy of Peru sent out a squadron in pursuit of Drake, but its commander, Luis de Toledo, apparently had no real desire to overtake him. At any rate Toledo was on his way home to Spain and ordered his ships to proceed direct to Panamá, where the "pursuit" ended.

On March 16, 1579, the "Golden Hind" and a small tender, or pinnace, arrived at Caño Island, an uninhabited rock off San Pedro Point in southern Costa Rica. Opposite the island, in a small bay on the deserted coast (probably Sierpe Bay[9]), Drake took the "Golden Hind" in to shore and proceeded to have her hull caulked, by shifting about the recently-taken ballast of silver bars in the hold. Meanwhile the pinnace with thirty men stood guard behind Caño Island, and on March 20 a small bark was sighted coming down from the

---

[9] Hydrographic Office, *Sailing Directions,* 221. There is another Caño Island nearby at the entrance to the Gulf of Nicoya (*ibid.,* 214), but the descriptions given apply more closely to the island off San Pedro Point.

north. This ship had left San Pedro del Palmar in the Gulf of Nicoya three days before, and was bound for Panamá with a crew of thirteen and a cargo of maize, honey, sarsaparilla, and lumber. Drake's pinnace ran out to intercept the Spanish ship, using both sails and oars, and amazed the enemy by calling on them to surrender with a flourish of trumpets and harquebuses fired in the air. At first the Spaniards did not know what to make of this racket, but when the pirates hit two of their men with harquebus balls they swiftly surrendered and were boarded.[10]

The prize was taken into the bay and examined by Drake, who treated the prisoners courteously, being especially pleased to find that two pilots of the Manila galleons, Alonso Sánchez Colchero and Martín de Aguirre, were aboard as passengers. Among their luggage were charts and sailing directions for the Manila-Acapulco route, eagerly confiscated by Drake. The Spaniards were horrified when one of the pirates smashed their ship's crucifix and kicked it into the sea.

Now Drake, in order to lighten the "Golden Hind" and at the same time give her protection while she was being worked on, had her guns and part of the silver ballast moved to the prize. The

---

[10] This is the only recorded instance when Spaniards were physically injured by Drake's men on the North American part of his cruise, if we except the ducking he subsequently gave a Manila pilot (see below). Drake's men swore that no Spaniard was killed on the entire voyage.

latter must have been a sturdy little ship, as Drake kept her with him for four months. The pirates continued caulking and trimming their vessel and taking on water, wood, and fish. On March 25 the guns were remounted in Drake's ship and she sailed out past Caño Island with the prize in tow. The prisoners, with the exception of the elderly pilot Sánchez Colchero, were given Drake's pinnace in which to make their way back to the Gulf of Nicoya.

Notice of Drake's presence now traveled somewhat slowly up the coast. The freed prisoners reached Esparza on March 29, and a coasting ship was dispatched to the port of Realejo, arriving there April 6. One of the *oidores* of the *audiencia* of Guatemala happened to be at Realejo and took charge of the place's defense. A breastwork was thrown up near the mouth of the creek, and a log chain was prepared to block access by boat to the town and shipyard, the most important place on the west coast of Central America. At the same time the warning about Drake was sent on by ship to Acajutla and thence to Guatemala, Guatulco, Acapulco, and Mexico City. The president of the *audiencia* of Guatemala, Licenciado Valverde, wrote on April 14 that he was getting together a fleet of three ships with two hundred men, and was having the church bells of Guatemala City melted down for cannon. He hoped to be ready to catch Drake on his return south.

But the enemy's progress was swifter than that of the Spanish messengers. While Realejo was preparing for an attack Drake had already passed by, having failed to induce the pilot, Sánchez Colchero, to lead him into that harbor. For his refusal the old man was ducked from the "Golden Hind's" yardarm.[11] Drake's next exploit was the capture of another Spanish vessel of about sixty tons bound from Acapulco to Peru with a cargo of Chinese merchandise. The two ships almost collided shortly before dawn on April 4, two leagues offshore north of Acajutla. On being hailed angrily by the Spaniards, Drake answered, also in Spanish, and simultaneously sent a boarding party which took the prize without resistance. It seems that nearly everyone on the Spanish ship was asleep, including the owner, a wealthy merchant and grandee named Francisco de Zárate. The Spaniards were rudely awakened, deprived of their rapiers and keys, and made prisoners in the hold of their own ship. Zárate was taken across to the "Golden Hind" and brought before Drake, whom he found pacing the quarterdeck. Drake was courteous, almost cordial, and invited his noble prisoner into the richly furnished cabin where he proceeded to quiz him about his cargo. There was very little gold or silver, only a quantity

---

[11] According to Peralta, *Costa-Rica Nicaragua y Panamá*, 588, Sánchez Colchero also refused 1,000 *ducados* which Drake offered to pay him if he continued as pilot across the Pacific.

of silks and cotton garments, chinaware, and a fine golden falcon with a large emerald embedded in its chest. Zárate was quite impressed with the courtly behavior of his captor and the furnishings of the pirate ship, but more particularly with the discipline and deference shown Drake by his officers.[12] That evening Drake added to the impression by having Zárate and Sánchez Colchero (now recovered from his ducking) to dine with him in his cabin. The food was excellent and served on fine English plate, with the usual musicians accompanying the meal.

The "Golden Hind" towed Zárate's ship for two days and nights, during which time Drake's men helped themselves to that part of the cargo which was valuable and not too bulky. On relieving Zárate of his golden falcon and other items Drake courteously apologized and explained that he merely wished to take home some souvenirs to his wife. In return he presented Zárate with a curved dagger and a silver chafing dish. On the morning of April 6, Zárate's ship was returned to him, while a handful of silver coins was distributed among the Spanish sailors and passengers to console them in their misfortune. Sánchez Colchero was also released at this time, but another pilot

---

[12] Zárate's comments on the exaggerated respect paid Drake by his gentlemen companions (*e. g.*, they did not "sit or cover in [Drake's] presence without first being ordered once and even several times") makes one wonder whether they were not putting on a show to further impress the Spaniards.

from Zárate's ship was detained to guide Drake into Guatulco. According to one account, Drake also kept a "negro wench called Maria, which was afterward gotten with child between the captaine and his men pirats, and sett on a small iland to take her adventure." Then Zárate was permitted to go on his way (he reached Realejo on April 15), and the "Golden Hind," still accompanied by the small prize taken off Caño Island, proceeded northwesterly across the Gulf of Tehuantepec.

At ten in the morning of April 13, 1579 (Monday of Holy Week) Drake's two ships entered the tiny port of Guatulco. Once the flourishing terminus of trade between Mexico and Peru, by 1579 Guatulco was being eclipsed by the rising port of Acapulco and was in a state of decline. In any event the period from April to June was a dead season for the Peruvian trade because of contrary winds. On Drake's arrival the port had a single ship of about one hundred tons at anchor. There were a handful of Spaniards, four or five hundred Indians, a collection of thatched huts and empty warehouses, and no fortification whatever. Moreover the news of Drake's presence in the Pacific had not yet reached Guatulco. The *alcalde mayor,* Gaspar de Vargas, at first thought the "Golden Hind" was "the ship from Peru that I was expecting," and he mistook the smaller prize for a local pearling vessel.[13] However an Italian sailor on the

---

[13] Letter from Vargas to the viceroy, April 13, 1579, in *México* 1254, AGI.

beach commented that they looked like Englishmen to him, so the Spaniards armed themselves
and got together some Indians for possible hostilities. As soon as he had dropped anchor Drake sent
ashore a launch with twenty-five men armed with
harquebuses, swords, and shields. The prize pinnace followed close behind, firing her perriers.
Seeing that it was hopeless to resist such a force
Vargas and the others promptly retreated to the
woods behind the town, leaving only the priest and
two other Spaniards who were taken prisoner by
the pirates. Then Drake came ashore with more
men who proceeded to loot the town. Not much of
value was found, a few thousand pesos in gold and
silver, some jewelry and clothing, and a quantity of provisions and water casks which were
badly needed. One of the Spanish officials later
complained that the English had "carried off from
Guatulco the entire supply of Indian women's
blouses [huipiles]"! In a gesture typical of the
times, the pirates desecrated the little church and
destroyed all the images and crucifixes, taking
away vestments, ornaments, and even the church
bell. The Spanish ship at anchor was also seized,
rummaged, and her bowsprit and topsails cut off.

That evening on the "Golden Hind" Drake
attended to his mission of building up English
prestige in the eyes of the Spanish colonials. First
his prisoners, including the priest, were obliged to
witness a Protestant service, led by Drake himself,
with the ship's company and orchestra joining in

with gusto for the psalms. Then they were given a stately dinner, and afterward a boy of the ship's company danced for the guests. Drake engaged his prisoners in conversation (he seems to have spoken fair Spanish) and told them that the purpose of his voyage was to do as much harm as possible to King Philip and his viceroy in New Spain.[14] He further mentioned that he would continue punishing the Spaniards until he had collected the £2,000,000 taken from his cousin John Hawkins at Vera Cruz in 1568 (Drake commanded one of the ships in that ill-fated expedition). After this peroration the prisoners were taken to a well-furnished cabin and locked in for the night.

Next morning all prisoners were put ashore after pleading to be left some food, to which Drake agreed. On the night of April 15 a commission of Spaniards, one being the *encomendero* of Guatulco, Bernardino López,[15] paid a social call on the "Golden Hind," taking care to arrive after dinner so they would not violate their Lenten fast by eating heretic beef. They had a pleasant visit with Drake and went ashore for the night.

Late in the evening of Maundy Thursday, April 16, 1579, Drake's two ships weighed anchor and sailed out of Guatulco. Just before their departure a boat had gone across from the "Golden Hind"

---

[14] Drake missed no opportunity to send threats and insults to the viceroys of Peru and New Spain. Zárate dutifully transmitted a similar message.

[15] López was *encomendero*, not Gómez Rengifo as Wagner says. *Cf.* Paso y Troncoso, *Papeles de Nueva España*, IV, p. 247.

to the Spanish ship and dropped off a Portuguese pilot, Nuño da Silva, whom Drake had taken on in the Cape Verde Islands and who had served him well as an officer and navigator. It appears that da Silva had asked to be left ashore, but he was promptly seized by the Spaniards as a pirate and a heretic. Altogether he was treated very badly by the Inquisition, and some years later took his revenge by leading his own pirate expedition to America. According to da Silva's testimony Drake still had eighty men and eight boys when he left Guatulco, a loss of only one or two men since entering the Pacific.[16]

On the day of Drake's arrival in Guatulco the *alcalde mayor* had sent messengers overland to Mexico City and Acapulco, and soon the entire viceroyalty was thrown into a turmoil. Troops were rushed to Acapulco, to Guatulco, to Guatemala, and even to Vera Cruz on the Atlantic. One of the surviving prisoners of the Hawkins expedition, Miles Philips, accompanied as interpreter a body of two hundred soldiers ordered to Acapulco, where they embarked in a sixty-ton ship and two pinnaces and followed the coast south as far as Guatemala. Most of the gentlemen-soldiers became violently seasick and disembarked in Guatulco, to return by land. Valverde, president of the *audiencia* of Guatemala, had also equipped and manned his fleet which he sent northward in pur-

---

[16] This suggests the possibility that Drake suspected the causes of scurvy and took steps to prevent it.

suit of the pirates. The annual Manila galleon had
sailed some months previously and would not
return to Acapulco before November,[17] a fact well
known to Drake, but Acapulco at that time had no
fortification, and wild rumors as to the pirates'
whereabouts and intentions caused a panic in New
Spain. It was generally believed that a whole
squadron of enemy ships was cruising along the
coast.

While all this was going on Drake, having
stowed his cannon in the hold, headed far out into
the Pacific, some five hundred leagues in a west-
southwest direction from Guatulco, until he found
winds which took him northward to Upper California. His desire was to cross the Pacific to the
Spice Islands (Moluccas) as soon as possible, but
the season for a favorable westward sailing had
passed. Besides, the "Golden Hind" was in poor
condition and needed to be careened again. On
June 3, 1579, the weather suddenly turned cold
and the rigging was frozen in a drizzly rain.
According to Wagner, the northernmost point
reached was probably 40° N., about two hundred
miles west of Cape Mendocino. Then the two
ships were driven toward shore and anchored in
an exposed bay where they experienced alternating
squalls and fog. The mountains inland were covered with snow. Finally, on June 17 they made

---

[17] It arrived at Acapulco on November 2 (*México* 20, AGI).

FRANCIS DRAKE TAKING ABOARD LOOT AND PRISONERS AT GUATULCO
From an Eighteenth Century engraving.

port, either in what is now Drake's Bay or, according to a plausible theory, within San Francisco Bay itself.[18] There they remained over a month, during which time the "Golden Hind" was careened and overhauled, and friendly contact was had with the Indians. Drake, having been crowned king by the natives, took possession of the country for Queen Elizabeth and named it New Albion.

On July 23, 1579, the "Golden Hind" sailed from her California port and went to some rocky islands, perhaps the Farallones, where the men caught seals and birds for additional provisions. Finally on July 25 the little ship, having left behind the prize bark, started southwest across the Pacific. Drake was extremely fortunate in finding good winds at this time of year, and reached the Caroline Islands on October 13. In the East Indies trade relations were successfully established, and on September 26, 1580, the "Golden Hind" sailed back into Plymouth harbor well ballasted with Spanish silver and gold. Subsequently Drake was knighted by his queen, played a leading part in the defeat of the Spanish Armada, and died in the Caribbean in 1596.

Drake's raid caused the Spaniards to take certain steps theretofore deemed unnecessary in defense of their Pacific ports and shipping. While

---

[18] Power, "Portus Novae Albionis Rediscovered?", 10-12. The literature on Drake's activities in California is too voluminous to be cited here.

the "Golden Hind" was on her way home by way of the Orient, a possibility not seriously considered by the rulers of Spanish America, the viceroy of Peru sent Pedro Sarmiento de Gamboa south to the Straits of Magellan with the idea of perhaps catching Drake on his return, or in any case of establishing a fortress there to keep other pirates from entering the Pacific.[19] The existence of an alternate passage a few miles farther south around Cape Horn was not yet suspected, and in fact Sarmiento did succeed in fortifying the straits, in 1584, although the little colony was almost wiped out by starvation and was abandoned four years later. The next point to concern the Spanish authorities was the protection of the ships which carried huge quantities of silver bullion from Peru to Panama for transshipment to Spain. It was decided to send them under convoy with one or two well-armed escorts, the latter carrying the grandiloquent title of *Armada real de la Mar del Sur.* This convoy system, when it was adhered to, effectively prevented a repetition of the disastrous "Cacafuego" incident. Further to protect the silver shipments a number of cannon were installed at Panamá, facing the sea.

However, north of Panamá nothing whatever was done to fortify the ports or to protect the tremendously rich cargoes of silver carried by sea from Peru to Mexico. Even more surprising, the

---

[19] Burney, *Chronological History,* II, p. 2.

Manila galleons remained totally without defense. Trans-Pacific trade had greatly increased since its inception in 1573. By 1586 the amount of silver leaving Acapulco each year on the China-bound vessels was probably well in excess of 1,000,000 pesos,[20] and ten years later the annual total had reached 12,000,000 pesos.[21] Most of this came originally from Peru, in spite of repeated cédulas forbidding the sale of Chinese goods in that kingdom. It can be understood why the viceroys would hesitate to provide royal protection for this illegal trade between Peru and Mexico, but it is surprising that, eight years after Drake's incursion, no steps had been taken to protect the king's galleons and there was not a single cannon on the entire Mexican west coast.[22] There had been much talk of building a fort at Acapulco, but nothing had been done.[23] The viceroy of New Spain wrote the king at the beginning of 1587, thanking him for the news that two more expeditions of English warships were on their way to the Pacific, and stating placidly that the defenses of his kingdom were in good order. Furthermore, he pointed out, there was really nothing to attract pirates to the west coast of New Spain, since he had forbidden

---

[20] Letters from viceroy, April 10, 1581 and May 10, 1586, in *México* 20, AGI.

[21] Borah, *Colonial Trade*, 123.

[22] Letter from viceroy, October 30, 1587, in *México* 21, AGI: ". . . no tiene v. magd. Una pieza de artilleria con que puedan asegurarse estos puertos."

[23] Letter from viceroy, October 28, 1582, in *México* 20, AGI.

anyone to settle there! [24] This myopic attitude was
also evident in the vulnerability of the Manila
galleon. On the westbound voyage there were
usually some soldiers bound for the Philippines,
and occasionally a few cannon were carried. But
on her return trip to Acapulco every inch of deck
space on the unwieldy ship was taken up with
bundles of valuable cargo and there was no room
for artillery. When we consider that these galleons
always returned, unescorted and unarmed, by the
same route, closely following the coast from California to Acapulco, and that the English knew
about this and even had charts and sailing directions for the China route (a fact well known to the
Spaniards), it is somewhat difficult to excuse the
complacent and unworried views of the viceroy.
However, it must be remembered that he was also
responsible for the defense of the Gulf of Mexico
and the Caribbean, and piracy there was much
more of a problem than in the Pacific.[25]

From 1585 a state of open war existed between
Spain and England. With a well balanced com-
bination of patriotism and self-interest, and encouraged by the phenomenal success of Drake, two
groups of adventurers prepared early in 1586 to

---

[24] *Idem,* January 20, 1587, in *México* 21, AGI.

[25] *Idem,* May 10, 1586, in *México* 20, AGI, and October 28, 1587,
in *México* 21, AGI. Fernández Duro, *Armada Española,* III, pp. 395-396,
claims that the defenseless condition of the Pacific at this time, was the
fault not of the viceroys but of the king, who was unwilling to spend
money for fortifications or the maintenance of a defense fleet because
he considered foreign intrusions in that sea "a transitory evil."

repeat his exploit. George Clifford, Earl of Cumberland, outfitted two ships with two hundred men commanded by Robert Withrington and Christopher Lister, who were subsequently joined by two other vessels, one of them the property of Sir Walter Raleigh.[26] The second expedition, the only one to reach the Pacific, was prepared and commanded by Thomas Cavendish (often spelled Candish), a young gentleman born in comfortable circumstances in Suffolk county in 1560. Cavendish was a gay blade in Elizabeth's court who lived beyond his means, and who decided to turn privateer in order to recover his fortune. In spite of his gentle upbringing Cavendish was a harsher foe than the plebeian-born Drake. He seems to have been a competent navigator and a conscientious hydrographer. His skill in naval warfare is difficult to evaluate, since he never faced an enemy anywhere near his equal. He was just twenty-six years old at the start of the voyage with which we are concerned, having acquired nautical experience on a colonizing expedition to America in 1583-85.

Cavendish left Plymouth harbor on July 31, 1586,[27] with three ships and a total complement of 123 men, some of whom had been with Drake on

---

[26] Burney, *Chronological History*, II, pp. 62-63.

[27] The Gregorian calendar had been adopted by Spain in 1582, although it was not used in England until 170 years later. Consequently there is a difference of ten (before 1700) or eleven (after 1700) days between English and Spanish reckoning. For conformity, all dates will be given hereafter according to the Gregorian calendar (N.S.)

his cruise around the world.[28] The flagship "Desire" was of 120 tons burden and mounted a strong armament of twenty-nine brass and cast-iron guns and two small perriers *(lombardas pedreras),* probably bow chasers.[29] The second ship, "Content," was of only sixty tons. In addition there was a bark, "Hugh Gallant," which was purposely sunk off the coast of Ecuador because of the depletion of the crews. The object of Cavendish's expedition was a simple one, to ravage the enemy's ports and shipping and obtain plunder. In addition a good deal of hydrographical information was to be acquired on the voyage, and there was some furthering of trade relations with the East Indies.

A number of Cavendish's men were lost in an outbreak of scurvy off the coast of Africa, and they suffered much from lack of food and a difficult passage through the Straits of Magellan. They entered the Pacific on March 6, 1587, and proceeded to raid the coasts of Chile and Peru without obtaining a great deal of booty. Central America was sighted on July 11, at which time the crews of the two remaining ships numbered about one hundred men and boys, sixty on the "Desire" and forty on the "Content."

---

[28] The basic account of Cavendish's voyage was written by a participant, Francis Pretty, *The Admirable and Prosperous Voyage of the Worshipfull Master Thomas Candish* . . .

[29] "Relación . . . de como los corsarios ingleses tomaron el navio santa Ana," a long *expediente* drawn up in the *audiencia* of Guadalajara and consisting of testimony of the *Santa Ana* survivors, in *Patronato Real* 265, *ramo* 51, AGI. The Spanish estimate of Cavendish's armament may be exaggerated.

Meanwhile toward the end of May the viceroy of Peru wrote urgent warnings to both Panamá and Mexico advising that Cavendish was on his way north. The president of Panamá sent out his son, Cristóbal de Mendoza, with two ships in pursuit of the enemy, but he was almost two weeks behind them. The viceroy of New Spain did not receive the letter from Peru until mid-October, by which time the Englishmen had already fallen upon his defenseless kingdom.[30]

On July 19 Cavendish came up to a 120-ton Spanish ship off the port of Acajutla and seized her without difficulty. The prize was in ballast, but again the English were fortunate in capturing one of the Manila pilots, a Frenchman known as Miguel Sánchez. Upon being subjected to the customary torture, Sánchez informed Cavendish that two galleons were expected to arrive that year from the Orient. They could not reach New Spain before November, which left the English ample time to choose a convenient spot and lie in wait. Cavendish had just set fire to his first prize when another vessel was sighted and easily captured, on July 20. The second ship, most of whose crew escaped to shore, had just left Acajutla bound northward to spread the news of pirates on the coast. This ship was also burned, contrasting with Drake's practice of releasing his prizes.[31]

[30] Letter from viceroy, October 28, 1587, in *México* 21, AGI. *Gobernantes del Perú*, x, pp. 415-16; xi, pp. 130-32.
[31] *Ibid.* Pretty, *Voyage of Candish,* 813.

Since he was reasonably sure that news of his presence had not yet reached Mexico, Cavendish decided to follow Drake's example and raid the defenseless port of Guatulco. The English squadron anchored off the mouth of the Copalita River on August 5 and a pinnace was sent ahead with thirty men, arriving at Guatulco early the following morning. Although the port had further declined in importance since Drake's visit, it still had a few hundred inhabitants and a certain amount of local trade.[32] Moreover it was being used as a depot for Chinese merchandise brought around from Acapulco and illegally transshipped to Peru. Shortly before Cavendish's arrival two Peruvian ships had called there and exchanged a large amount of silver for Chinese goods. Juan de Rengifo, the new *alcalde mayor,* apparently profited from this contraband trade and consequently was quite pleased to see Cavendish's pinnace coming into the bay.[33] The only other ship in port at the time was a fifty-ton bark loaded with cacao from Acajutla.[34]

The first act of Cavendish's men was to make an easy prize of the cacao ship lying at anchor. Then they landed on the beach with a great racket of muskets and harquebuses and took the town without resistance. Rengifo was made prisoner while most of the inhabitants fled to the woods. There was very little to plunder. Cavendish's

---

[32] Gay, *Historia de Oaxaca,* II, p. 77.

[33] Murguía, "Estadística antigua," 192-193..

[34] Pretty, *op. cit.,* 814. *México* 21, AGI.

chronicler describes the place as having a hundred brush and wattle huts, a church, and a large customhouse filled with cacao and indigo. The church was desecrated and the whole town put to the torch.[35]

The following day, August 7, Cavendish came in with his two ships, disembarked, and took thirty men to raze the countryside for several miles around. Before leaving Guatulco the English burned the cacao bark and attempted to destroy a large wooden cross on the shore. According to the Spanish historians the "Santa Cruz" miraculously remained unscathed after the pirates attacked it with axes, saws and fire, and then tried to pull it loose with a line secured between it and their flagship.[36]

---

[35] Murguía, op. cit., 193-194. Pretty, op. cit., 814.

[36] It is difficult to separate fact from legend in the matter of this "Santa Cruz de Guatulco." Pretty does not mention the incident at all. It is briefly mentioned in a contemporary report from Peru (Gobernantes del Perú, XI, p. 132). The story is told in detail by Burgoa in Geográfica descripción, II, pp. 290 ff., who claims to have seen an expediente exceeding two thousand folios treating on the subject, drawn up about 1610 at the instance of the bishop of Oaxaca, and containing testimony of people who were in Guatulco at the time of Cavendish's attack. The matter is also discussed at length in Torquemada, Monarchia Indiana, 3a parte, 205-206. The cross was supposed to have been brought to Guatulco long before the conquest. After its miraculous preservation from the "heretic" pirates it was almost destroyed by souvenir collectors, and in 1612 or 1613 the bishop had it moved to Oaxaca. Smaller crosses were then made from the wood, one of which is still venerated in a chapel of the cathedral at Oaxaca. Many miracles were ascribed to this cross. It was supposed to be particularly effective in the cure of pregnancy disorders and speech impediments. The story of the pirate attack has been repeated and changed by subsequent writers, some of them confusing Cavendish with Drake and others.

Cavendish sailed from Guatulco on August 12 and ran up the coast past Acapulco. He knew there would be little incentive for a raid there, and suspected that the place might be defended. Probably he could have taken Acapulco, still without any fortification and at the moment almost without defenders. The news of Cavendish's presence did not reach Mexico City until the middle of August, when the viceroy took some feeble steps toward the protection of the west coast. He sent warnings to Guadalajara and other points, and ordered troops to Oaxaca and Acapulco. General Cristóbal de Mendoza, who is described as "very much of a youth and without any experience," finally reached the latter port with his pirate-hunting squadron early in October.[37] Two Mexican ships were ready to join this fleet and pursue Cavendish northward, but Mendoza procrastinated to such an extent that the viceroy appointed his own general to head the expedition, Diego García de Palacio, an *oidor* of the *audiencia* of Mexico. Then began a foolish quarrel between the two Spanish generals. Mendoza refused to give up his command and threatened to sack Acapulco for supplies. After warning García not to follow, as he wanted to capture the pirates by himself, Mendoza sailed off in the wrong direction back to Panamá. García left Acapulco with his two ships a day or so later and tried to sail to the northwest, but was forced back by contrary winds within a week. He made several

---

[37] Letter from viceroy, October 28, 1587, in *México* 21, AGI.

other attempts but never got beyond thirty leagues west of Acapulco.[38]

While this farce was being enacted Cavendish continued his depredations far to the north. On September 3 he sent his pinnace and thirty men in to the port of Navidad, following them within a few hours. There was a shipyard with a tiny settlement on the shore, Navidad being at the time headquarters of a pearling monopoly extending to California.[39] One of the pearling ships had recently sailed northward, but in the shipyard Cavendish destroyed two vessels of about 150 tons each. They were almost ready to be launched and belonged to Juan Toscano and Antonio del Castillo.[40] At Navidad the English also captured a messenger who carried the viceroy's warning of their presence, and set fire to the few shacks at the mouth of the lagoon.[41]

Two days later, on September 5, Cavendish weighed anchor and ran south to the deserted bays of Santiago and Salagua, where he remained a week taking on water. When this work was done the men amused themselves by swimming, fishing, and diving for pearls. On the thirteenth, they returned northward to "Malacca" Bay (probably

---

[38] *Idem,* January 15, 1588, in *México* 21, AGI.

[39] Gerhard, "Pearl Diving," 240.

[40] *México* 21, AGI.

[41] Pretty, *op. cit.,* 815. According to a report from the *audiencia* of Guadalajara dated September 23, 1587, that body had dispatched Luis de Carvajal with some soldiers to Navidad, but he got there after Cavendish had left (*México* 21, AGI.)

what is now known as Tenacatita Bay), one league west of Navidad. Here Cavendish took thirty men inland to the village of Acatlán, where they defaced the church and burned most of the houses.[42] Leaving Malacca on September 14 the two ships arrived four days later at the cove of Chacala, where they found two shacks on the beach. Another landing party spent a day unsuccessfully rummaging the countryside for provisions, of which they were very much in need. Finally they took a few prisoners and induced their wives to ransom them by bringing food down to the beach. Two of the prisoners were carried off by Cavendish when he left Chacala on September 20.[43]

A call of five days was made at the "Isle of St. Andrew," probably one of the Tres Marías, where some iguanas and birds were caught. On October 4 the English anchored in the uninhabited port of Mazatlán and took on more provisions, mostly fish. Finding his ships in need of repairs Cavendish next ran across to the islands just north of Mazatlán. The "Desire" and "Content" were careened and trimmed and the pinnace was "new-built" in the twelve days they remained there. One of the prisoners made his escape by swimming a mile to the mainland, while another saved the day by showing the pirates where to dig for fresh water when their supply was almost exhausted. At one point a troop of some thirty or forty horsemen

[42] Pretty, *loc. cit.*
[43] *Ibid.*

appeared on the opposite shore. They were probably from the new presidio of Mazatlán, fourteen miles inland.[44]

On October 19 the little fleet sailed from Mazatlán and in five days crossed the mouth of the gulf to Cape San Lucas, at the southern tip of Lower California, where Cavendish had determined to wait for the Manila galleons. They took shelter in the little bay behind the cape, where they found "a fayre riuer of fresh water, with great store of fresh fish, foule, and wood, and also many hares and conies." One of the ships was kept cruising off the cape, and sentinels were stationed on the hills overlooking the Pacific.[45]

Two galleons were crossing from the Philippines to Acapulco in 1587, the "Nuestra Señora de Esperanza" and the "Santa Ana." The pilot of the first of these ships, Pedro de Unamuño, had been instructed to make certain explorations, and spent some time cruising about the North Pacific looking for the legendary islands of Rica de Oro, Rica de Plata, and Isla del Armenio. He landed in Upper California, made a trip inland, and then followed the coast southward, rounding Cape San

---

[44] *Ibid.* Olea, "Historia de Mazatlán." Pretty thought the horsemen were from Chametla.

[45] Pretty, *op. cit.,* 816-817. Some writers have suggested that Cavendish's "Aguada Segura" was the roadstead of San José del Cabo rather than San Lucas Bay, but the report of a pearler who visited and clearly identified San Lucas Bay in 1632 clears up the doubt (Carbonel MS.). Carbonel says they found pieces of chinaware on the beach, left over from the visit of the "yngles corsario llamado tomas candi." San José del Cabo has a completely unsheltered roadstead.

Lucas early in November. Apparently he was too far off the Cape to be sighted by Cavendish's lookouts. On November 12 Unamuño reached Banderas Bay where he met a launch which had been sent out from Navidad with orders to cross to California and warn the galleons about the pirates. However, the launch had been unable to get across the gulf.[46]

The second galleon, "Santa Ana," recently built at Realejo, had made only one trip to the Orient.[47] She was of about 700 English tons burden, extremely unwieldy and slow, and on her fatal voyage she carried no armament except a few rusty muskets and harquebuses. Furthermore her decks were so crowded with bales of cargo that there was scarcely room for the crew and passengers, who numbered more than three hundred at the start of the voyage. She was commanded by Tomás de Alzola, and among the merchants aboard was the future general and explorer, Sebastián Vizcaíno.

In the evening of November 14, 1587, more than four months out of Manila, the "Santa Ana" came slowly up to Cape San Lucas.[48] Her lookout saw

---

[46] Almost identical accounts of Unamuño's voyage appear in two *legajos* of *Patronato Real:* 25, *ramo* 32; and 260, *ramo* 14; AGI.

[47] *México* 20, AGI.

[48] There are certain minor discrepancies between the English and Spanish versions of this battle. The former is found in Pretty, *op. cit.*, 816-817; the latter in *Patronato Real* 265, *ramo* 51, AGI. Where they differ, this writer follows the Spanish account, particularly Alzola's detailed statement. Pretty says that the battle took place on November 4 (14, N. S.), and that the Spaniards set out a flag of truce after the third attack. He has the "Santa Ana" towed into port on November 6 (16, N. S.).

two sails on the horizon, but Alzola assumed they were Spanish vessels, perhaps pearlers. The following morning, however, Cavendish's two ships and pinnace were clearly visible and were recognized as enemies. As the English bore down on the galleon Alzola called together his crew and passengers, distributed such arms as could be found (muskets, harquebuses, swords, lances, and rocks), and assigned each man a place behind one of a series of improvised shields. After a chase of several hours the "Desire" came up and at close quarters began to fire her great guns and a barrage of small shot into the "Santa Ana." Then she grappled against the galleon amidship on the starboard side, and some forty men managed to board the Spanish vessel in spite of a hail of rocks dumped on them from the higher deck of the "Santa Ana." There was a confused moment of close fighting, during which Alzola shot down one of Cavendish's officers who had climbed up to the mainsail yard and was doing great damage hacking away at the stays and rigging. In this initial assault the English lost two dead and several wounded, and were forced to retreat.

Now the "Desire" moved off to reload her guns and came in for a second attack. This time no attempt was made to board, but the guns were fired at such short range that they did a great deal of damage, killing and maiming many of the Spaniards. A third time the "Desire" moved in, grappling with the "Santa Ana" near the bow. Again the English succeeded in boarding the enemy, and again they were repulsed after heavy fighting. It was now clear to Cavendish that the "Santa Ana," with no artillery to strike back, could be subdued more easily with his guns than by hand-to-hand combat. The fourth attack was the final one. All the English artillery was brought into play, and after an hour or so the defenseless "Santa Ana" could take no more. Splintered masts and rigging were heaped on her deck and the sea was pouring in through gaping holes at the waterline. Many of the Spaniards had been killed, nearly all were wounded, and they had no more powder. A boat was lowered and rowed over to the "Desire" with a flag of truce. Cavendish sent word to Alzola to strike those sails which were still aloft and come aboard with his officers, and the order was obeyed.

In addition to the usual cargo of Chinese goods, silks and other fine cloths, perfumes, spices, chinaware, and quantities of wine and provisions, the "Santa Ana" was carrying a fortune in specie. There were 122,000 pesos in gold coin and a number of fine pearls. On November 17 the galleon was towed into San Lucas Bay and a careful inventory was made of the great treasure. On the nineteenth the Spanish survivors, numbering 190 and including some women, were stripped of their personal possessions "without leaving them a single pin" and put ashore. Cavendish gave them their ruined sails for tents, and a few provisions. Later Alzola was released and set ashore with arms and

powder for defense against the Indians, who had
been watching the strange white men with great
interest. Alzola was also given the "Santa Ana's"
cargo register, at the end of which was a receipt
thoughtfully signed by Cavendish! The English
kept eight prisoners: the galleon's pilot, a Portuguese merchant, two Japanese boys, three young
Filipinos, and a priest named Juan de Almen-
dáriz. The latter had offended Cavendish in some
way, and he was hanged from the mainmast yard
and his body thrown into the sea. The others were
taken aboard the "Desire."

On the same day (the nineteenth) there was a
near mutiny among the English seamen. The men
of the "Content" particularly, who seem to have
had little or no part in the fighting, complained
loudly over the division of spoils, but they were
soon pacified. According to the Spanish account
the treasure finally was divided into three equal
parts, two for Cavendish and one to be spread
among the others. For over a week the "Santa
Ana" was thoroughly rummaged of the most valuable part of her cargo, and still there was a great
deal (Pretty says five hundred tons) which had to
be left behind.

On November 29, 1587, the English destroyed
what remained of the "Santa Ana's" masts and
stays and set her afire. With a proud salvo the
"Desire" sailed out of the port, trailed by the
"Content," the pinnace having been taken aboard
the flagship. The "Content" fell behind, heading

in a more northerly direction, and was never heard from again. Cavendish eventually fell in with the normal westward route of the Manila ships and reached Guam in only forty-five days. The "Desire" went on to the Philippines and the East Indies, rounded South Africa, and arrived in Plymouth harbor with her treasure intact on September 20, 1588.

Marooned at San Lucas and already on a bad footing with the primitive Indians, the survivors from the "Santa Ana" watched their wreck drift inshore and continue burning, half sunk, for two days. Little remained but the keel and part of the timbers. With considerable dexterity the Spaniards salvaged what they could, removed the ballast, and somehow got the "Santa Ana" into such condition that they were able to sail her once again. They left San Lucas on December 21, taking with them two California Indians (a man and a woman). They not only managed to reach the mainland, but continued down the coast to Acapulco, where they arrived on January 7, 1588.[49]

The loss of the Manila ship was a humiliating and costly blow to Spain. It caused the ruin of many merchants and a widespread if temporary depression which was felt throughout New Spain. Shortly before Cavendish returned to Plymouth,

[49] *Patronato Real* 265, *ramo* 51, AGI. Venegas, *Noticia de la California,* III, p. 37.

Spain's great invading Armada had been repelled in the English Channel with heavy losses. With England in control of the sea it was natural to expect further enemy incursions in the Pacific, but in spite of this danger the west coast of New Spain was to remain totally undefended for thirty years more. While the memory of Cavendish's raid was fresh the viceroy wrote earnestly of moving cannon down to the coast, but there is no sign that this was done.[50] The Manila trade increased tenfold in ten years, and still the clumsy galleons were without defense on their return voyage to Mexico. They even omitted the sensible precaution, ordered many times by the viceroys, of keeping well out to sea until they reached the latitude of Acapulco. The only other suggestion offered by several of the viceroys was to keep the whole Pacific shore, with the exception of Acapulco, depopulated, in order to make pirate visits unprofitable. This theory continued in vogue for many years, and may well be one of the reasons that the west coast of Mexico is so sparsely inhabited today.[51]

In June, 1588, word of pirates on the coast of Chile reached Mexico, and the viceroy sent two ships to Cedros Island to escort the Manila galleons.[52] The rumor was a false one, but the follow-

---

[50] Letter from viceroy, January 15, 1588, in *México* 21, AGI.

[51] In *México* 24, AGI, is much evidence that the galleons continued to sight Cedros Island and San Lucas, and followed the coast from Cape Corrientes to Acapulco.

[52] Letters from viceroy, January 15 and June 30, 1588, in *México* 21, AGI.

ing year an expedition did in fact leave England for the South Sea. It was commanded by Andrew Merick and sailed from Plymouth in August, 1589, being forced back by contrary winds in the Straits of Magellan. Thomas Cavendish started out on another raiding voyage in 1591, but his ship also found the passage through the straits too difficult. The famed privateer died at the age of thirty-two on his way home through the Atlantic.[53] In the spring of 1594 the last of the Elizabethans to roam the Pacific, Richard Hawkins, sailed through the straits and proceeded to ravage shipping and coastal settlements in Chile and Peru. His ship was inappropriately named "Dainty." [54] Warning was sent on to Mexico, and at the end of August the viceroy ordered Alonso de Arellano to take a ship and pinnace from Acapulco northward to alert the China galleon.[55] Meanwhile Hawkins had been captured by the Spaniards off the coast of Ecuador in July.

As the war with England dragged on, rumors and illusions of enemy ships in the Pacific continued to trouble the Spaniards. In October, 1597, some Indian fishermen at Mazatlán reported having seen three "English" vessels bound for Cape San Lucas. The viceroy immediately dispatched General Sebastián Vizcaíno, again to protect the galleons. Vizcaíno got to San Lucas with consider-

---

[53] Burney, *Chronological History*, II, pp. 95-107.
[54] [Hawkins], *Observations*, 110-180.
[55] Letter from viceroy, October 25, 1594, in *México* 22, AGI.

able difficulty but did not see the pirates, nor did he meet the galleons, all three of which safely arrived in Acapulco the following February.[56] On her return voyage in 1598 the Manila ship "San Gerónimo" sighted what were thought to be three enemy sails off Cedros Island in early October. The passengers and crew swore that the pirate ships, about two leagues distant, were clearly visible. Still another sail on the horizon appeared to be the second Manila galleon, "Santa Margarita," which the Spaniards assumed had been captured, since all four ships chased the "San Gerónimo" until they were outdistanced. When this alarming news reached the viceroy he sent two companies of soldiers to Acapulco and prepared to dispatch a rescue fleet, but before they could sail the "Santa Margarita" arrived in port unscathed. Her captain stated that he had followed orders and did not even sight Cedros Island. The viceroy theorized that perhaps some clouds had been mistaken for ships.[57]

The English were not to sail again on the west coast for many years, but a new scourge was soon to appear in the form of certain hardy Dutch navigators, also enemies of Spain.

[56] *Real Orden* of June 3, 1607, in *Guadalajara* 36; also, letter from viceroy, February 26, 1598, in *México* 24, AGI.

[57] Letters from viceroy, December 13, 1598 and June 8, 1599, in *México* 24, AGI.

III
The Pechelingues

The Pechelingues

Since her revolt from Spanish rule in 1566, Holland had joined England and France in attacking Spanish ships both in Europe and America. The northern Netherlands had become a strong manufacturing nation in need of markets. In addition the Dutch were fanatically Protestant, bitterly resenting Philip II's harsh methods of fighting their rebellion. In the 1570s Holland's experienced and hardy seamen began to win renown under the name of Sea Beggars, and soon the tiny country had a merchant marine whose blond captains and sailors rivaled and in some ways surpassed the other European nations in nautical skill and acquaintance with the far corners of the earth. First in Europe and later in Spanish America the Dutch raiders came to be known to the Spaniards as Flexelingas, or Pechelingues, a word which has been traced to the name of their island port of Vlissingen, or Flushing.[1]

In 1595 Holland formed an alliance with France and England against Spain, and the Dutch States

---

[1] Sluiter, "The word Pechelingue."

General made plans for carrying the war to the Spanish colonies in the Pacific. The first expedition to leave Holland for the west coast of America was armed and commissioned by the States General and financed by a company of Dutch merchants. The joint commanders, Jacob Mahu and Simon de Cordes, had a fleet of five ships, some as large as six hundred tons, with total crews of nearly five hundred men. They carried a large stock of merchandise for contraband trade, and over one hundred guns. The squadron sailed from Rotterdam at the end of June, 1598, and proceeded to West Africa and the Straits of Magellan, where they were obliged to spend the winter. By the time they reached the Pacific, in September, 1599, the crews had taken such punishment from scurvy, hunger, and cold that only three hundred men survived. Mahu died in the Atlantic, and Cordes and fifty of his men were killed by the Araucanians in southern Chile. As a final blow to the Dutch plans, the viceroy of Peru had been forewarned and had a squadron of five warships ready to repel the intruders. The smallest of the Dutch vessels surrendered voluntarily to the Spaniards. Two others sailed from Chile in November, 1599, to cross the Pacific, and the remaining ship succeeded in capturing a few Spanish prizes before leaving the coast of Peru in June, 1600, also to make her way toward Asia.[2]

---

[2] Sluiter MS., "The Dutch on the Pacific Coast," 109-190. Burney, *Chronological History*, II, pp. 186-199.

Somewhat more successful was the smaller expedition led by Olivier van Noort, who left Rotterdam three months after Mahu and Cordes. His squadron, composed of two large ships and two *jachts* or small pursuit vessels, was fitted out by the Magellan Company, a Dutch trading concern, and sailed in September, 1598. Scurvy broke out almost at the start of the voyage, and bad weather punished the crews. When van Noort reached the Pacific at the end of February, 1600, his fleet consisted of the flagship, "Mauritius"; the "Hendrick Fredrick," commanded by Pieter Esaiasz. de Lint; and the smaller "Eendracht." The two larger ships were of about 250-300 tons each, and the *jacht* of about fifty tons. The "Mauritius" had twenty-four guns and a crew of some seventy men and boys, among whom was an English pilot who had served with Cavendish. De Lint's ship was slightly smaller with seventeen guns (ten cast-iron and seven brass) and a crew of about sixty.[3]

Van Noort and de Lint were separated on March 12, 1600, in southern Chile, and did not see each other again. The "Mauritius" had taken a few prizes at Valparaíso and was cruising off Peru when news of the viceroy's recently assembled defense squadron reached van Noort. He abandoned his original plan of going on to California, and determined to keep well out to sea until he

---

[3] Sluiter MS. 111-124. Details of de Lint's ship are from the letter of Fr. Agustín de Cavallos, September 2, 1600, in *México* 24, AGI.

found a good wind to take him across the Pacific. It would seem that the "Mauritius" turned west in the latitude of Panamá in May, after searching vainly for Cocos Island, and sailed across to the Philippines. There van Noort sank a Spanish ship which had been sent out to capture him, and eventually reached Holland in August, 1601.[4]

At the same time that van Noort was passing the latitude of Callao, the viceroy's nephew, Juan de Velasco, was preparing to take his five warships from that port to Panamá with several million pesos in silver.[5] Velasco waited until the bullion had been carried safely across the isthmus and then cruised slowly north along the coast, with three galleons and a *patache* (sloop), all well armed and carrying four hundred men. On his arrival at Acapulco on July 26 Velasco wrote the viceroy of New Spain expressing his belief that the pirates were already on their way across the Pacific. He had "counted the stones along the coast" from Panamá north, and had found no trace of the enemy.[6] However he had been ordered to proceed as far as Cape San Lucas, so the squadron left Acapulco on August 13 and spent ten days at the tip of California. On its return southward Velasco's fleet ran into a hurricane off Salagua which

---

[4] Sluiter MS., pp. 154-157.

[5] *Ibid.*, 158. Fernández Duro, *Armada Española*, III, pp. 262-266. It is interesting to note that the *almiranta* of Velasco's fleet was Hawkins's old ship "Dainty," now nicknamed "La Inglesa."

[6] Letter from Velasco, July 26, 1600, in *México 24*, AGI.

did great damage to the Spanish warships. Velasco and his flagship, in fact, were never seen again. The remaining vessels limped into Acapulco without their commander at the end of September, refitted, and went north a second time on November 4 to look for Velasco and the pirates. After eight weeks in this fruitless search they returned to Acapulco, and finally sailed back to Peru in February, 1601. The cruise was not a total loss, as they carried home a quantity of contraband Chinese merchandise.[7]

While the Peruvian fleet patrolled the west coast, the viceroy of New Spain took his own steps to protect the three Manila galleons expected in Acapulco. He ordered out the few available vessels, including a small ship from Chacala which reached San Lucas on December 1, the same day that the first of the galleons arrived at Acapulco. The other two came into port in January, 1601. They had been warned about the Dutch and had kept thirty leagues off Cape San Lucas.[8]

Meanwhile the partial cause of all this concern, de Lint in the vice-admiral "Hendrick Fredrick," took several prizes off Chile and Peru and arrived at uninhabited Coiba Island at the beginning of August, 1600. Here he spent several days taking on water, plantains, and wood. On August 11 he

---

[7] *México* 24, AGI. Letter from *alcalde mayor* of Acapulco, April 16, 1601, in *México* 371, AGI. Fernández Duro, *Armada Española*, III, p. 266.

[8] *México* 24, AGI.

came up to a small vessel bound from Nicoya to Panamá with a cargo of maize, becalmed off Caño Island. De Lint sent two boatloads of men to capture the prize, whereupon the Spaniards tried to escape in their ship's boat, but they were soon overtaken. The Spanish bark carried a passenger, a Franciscan priest named Agustín de Cavallos, who left an account of his brief stay among the "heretics," which is nearly all the information we have about de Lint's cruise. According to Cavallos, the Dutch crew numbered fifty-four men, many of whom spoke good Spanish. De Lint had a copy of Cavendish's log and said he planned to cruise north and careen his ship at Cape San Lucas. He expected to rendezvous there with van Noort, perhaps capture a galleon, and then cross to the Moluccas and China. It seems quite likely that this information was given Cavallos to mislead the Spaniards.[9]

On August 27, after a second visit to Coiba, de Lint was again off Caño Island and captured a small bark out of Costa Rica loaded with provisions and belonging to Pedro Gonzales, a Portuguese. She had a crew of sixteen, including a Dutchman and three Negroes whom de Lint kept on his ship. The rest of the prisoners, among them Fr. Cavallos, were stripped of their clothing and

---

[9] Letters from Fr. Agustín de Cavallos (Nicoya, September 2, 1600) and the president of the *audiencia* (Guatemala, November 23, 1600), in *México* 24, AGI. *Cf.* Sluiter, "New Light from Spanish Archives."

possessions and set ashore south of Realejo on August 29.[10]

Just where the "Hendrick Fredrick" spent the next few months after putting ashore her prisoners is somewhat of a mystery. She was not seen again on the coast of New Spain nor anywhere else in America. It was not until April or May, 1601, that de Lint appeared at Ternate, in the Molucca Islands. The crossing should not have taken more than three or four months, and it is interesting to speculate whether de Lint might not have gone after all to a secluded bay in Lower California, or more likely to Cocos Island, to careen his ship before starting across the Pacific.[11]

After de Lint's departure, Mexico was to have a respite of fifteen years before the Pechelingues returned to the Pacific. Philip III was too involved in his European wars to give much thought or encouragement to the defense of the Pacific coast, but the viceroy of New Spain took the initiative of sending a few cannon from Puebla the long way via Tehuantepec to Acapulco in 1601.[12] Two years

[10] Ibid.

[11] Fifteen years later Speilbergen vainly searched for Cocos, "for the reason that said island is very convenient, and offers advantages for revictualling, as some of our men knew from their own experience" (Speilbergen, East and West Indian Mirror, 102). This would seem to indicate that de Lint did indeed call there, and that some of his crew later sailed with Speilbergen.

[12] Letter from viceroy, November 1, 1601, in México 24, AGI.

later a Dutch captain with the picturesque nick-
name of Swarthy Tony, alias Black Anthony,
made a raid far to the south in Chile, but we do
not know whether the news of his exploits reached
Mexico.[13] In 1609 the war between Holland and
Spain officially came to an end, and those responsible for the safety of the Peruvian silver ships and
the Manila galleons heaved a sigh of relief and
grew careless. The impossibility of stopping the
highly lucrative trade between Mexico and Peru
was recognized, and after 1609 two ships carrying
a total of 300,000 pesos in silver were legally
allowed to sail each year, unescorted, from Callao
to Acapulco.[14] In addition there was still a considerable amount of contraband in Chinese goods,
mostly paid for with Peruvian bullion. At this ripe
moment the Dutch, in violation of their truce with
Spain, prepared to send a large military expedition
to the Pacific.

News of the latest danger reached Mexico City
at the end of 1614. In August of that year the
Dutch East India Company dispatched a fleet of
four large warships and two *jachts* on a "trading
mission" around the world by way of the South
Sea. Their announced intention was to offer Dutch
merchandise for sale in Spanish America. If the
Spanish authorities chose to deny them the facility
of free trade (as they undoubtedly would) the

---

13 Burney, *Chronological History*, III, pp. 17-18.
14 Borah, *Colonial Trade*, 127.

Dutchmen were instructed to protect their nation's interests by force and to repel and retaliate to any hostile act. The peaceful nature of the enterprise was at once belied by the strong armament of the Dutch ships, and it was quite clear that the Spanish colonials were in for another round of piracy in the Pacific.[15]

The leader of the Dutch squadron was a veteran navigator and sea fighter, Admiral Joris van Speilbergen. Born in 1568, Speilbergen had already participated in privateering enterprises to Africa, America, and the Far East, and had a prominent role in defeating the Spaniards at the battle of Gibraltar in 1607. He maintained strict discipline on his ships but seems to have been more than usually solicitous of the health and well-being of his men. Like Drake, he was a seasoned diplomat with a knowledge of the sort of show and flourish which created an impression of strength and opulence and enhanced his country's prestige in foreign ports. His flagship was tastefully furnished and well supplied with wines and delicacies, the officers' meals being accompanied by an orchestra and chorus of mariners. On ceremonial occasions the men were dressed smartly in full and gaudy uniform. At the start of the voyage there were some eight hundred men and boys on the six vessels,

---

[15] The authority on this expedition is the journal of Speilbergen, *East and West Indian Mirror*. Additional details are found in the Sluiter MS., 172-228.

mostly Netherlanders from Zeeland and the Fris-
ian Islands with a sprinkling of German, French,
English, and Irish. They were about evenly
divided between sailors and soldiers.[16]

The largest of Speilbergen's ships were the
"Groote Sonne" and the "Groote Maane," admiral
and vice-admiral respectively, of about six hundred
tons each. Second-in-command of the squadron
was Claes Martensz. Thoveling. Each of these
ships carried twenty-eight guns, most of cast iron
but some of brass, with the usual perriers and
plenty of ammunition and small arms. The latter
included new muskets, fireballs, grenades, both
long and short pikes, and broadswords. The "Morgensterre" and the "Aeolus" were of four hundred
tons and twenty-four guns each. The *jachts,*
"Jager" and "Meeuwe," had a burden of about
one hundred tons and carried eight to twelve guns
each.[17] In each of the larger ships were a master,
four pilots, a captain of soldiers, a cartographer,
and one or more factors or trade agents. Stowed
away about the decks were ten longboats, used as
galleys, each capable of carrying fifty to sixty men
and mounting two or three bow chasers. According
to Sluiter, the larger vessels were comparable in

---

[16] Speilbergen, *op. cit., passim.* Sluiter MS., 178-179.

[17] *Ibid.* The number of cannon is from Sluiter. However, according
to a Spanish report made in Acapulco, "El Sol" ["Groote Sonne"]
had 48 guns, "La Luna" ["Groote Maane"] 38, "La Estrella Rotra-
dama" ["Morgensterre"] 20, "Nao Peche Linga" ["Aeolus"] 24, and
"El Yagre" ["Jager"] 14. Letter from viceroy, October 28, 1615, in
México 28, AGI.

size to the Spanish galleons but lacked their high poops and forecastles. The ships' hulls were double-sheathed for protection against the teredo.

That the Speilbergen expedition was in part a trading voyage is apparent from the lading papers, which list a considerable quantity of merchandise and silver coin, quite apart from the usual provisions. However, this cargo was not intended for trade in Spanish America but was to be exchanged for Oriental products in the East Indies, where the Dutch were beginning to establish trading factories. The chief object of the whole voyage was to add the strength of Speilbergen's fleet to other Dutch forces in the Moluccas in order to repel a powerful Spanish squadron which was being prepared in the Philippines to expel the Dutch from Indonesia.[18] Long before Speilbergen reached Spanish waters there are references in his journal to warlike preparations for dealing with the Spanish "enemy." Probably his secret orders provided for the capture of the Manila galleon and any other Spanish ship when the opportunity arose, and the raiding and pillaging of Spanish-American ports. Speilbergen held a commission from the States General and Prince Mauritius of Orange. His orders, while giving the admiral supreme command of the expedition, provided for a "broad council" composed of the principal officers of the squadron, which met frequently and

[18] Speilbergen, *op. cit.,* 80.

acted as an advisory body. It also functioned, when occasion arose, as an admiralty court.[19]

Leaving Holland in August, 1614, the Dutch fleet crossed to Brazil and entered the Pacific through the Straits of Magellan in early May of the following year. The *jacht* "Meeuwe" had deserted, and further losses from scurvy and a scrape with the Portuguese reduced the Dutch force to some seven hundred men in four ships and a single *jacht*. Off the coast of Chile, Speilbergen learned that the forewarned Spaniards had assembled a powerful defense squadron in Peru. It was commanded by Don Rodrigo de Mendoza and consisted of eight ships manned with some thirteen hundred officers, soldiers, and sailors, but with less artillery than the Dutch. Speilbergen and his council decided, rather than avoid combat, to attack this formidable fleet. In a remarkable twenty-four-hour engagement off Cañete, Peru (July 17-18, 1615) the Dutch achieved a complete victory in which the Spaniards lost two warships and some four hundred fifty dead. Only forty of Speilbergen's men were killed, while his ships were practically unharmed.[20]

The whole west coast of America now lay helpless before the Pechelingues. Sailing north, Speilbergen put in at Paita, which was burned to the ground when its inhabitants fled with their belong-

[19] *Ibid., passim.*
[20] *Ibid.,* 11-77.

ings. In late August, 1615, the Dutch fleet sailed from the South American mainland in a vain search for Cocos Island, and on September 20 they first sighted the coast of Central America in the vicinity of Amapala.[21]

As mentioned above, the authorities in New Spain had received the news of Speilbergen's departure from Europe, and his proposed itinerary, toward the end of 1614. In January of the following year the viceroy ordered the *alcalde mayor* of Acapulco to strengthen the defenses of that port. Trenches were dug and gun emplacements erected on the hill of El Morro on the north side of the inner harbor. Fourteen guns were hauled down from the interior and mounted beside the three old cannon which theretofore constituted the sole armament. Don Melchor Fernández de Córdoba, a nobleman and relative of the viceroy, was commissioned general in charge of South Sea defenses and reached Acapulco with troops in March, remaining there until the two galleons were on their way to the Philippines. When word of the pirates' activities in Peru reached Mexico in September, Acapulco was again deserted, but Fernández returned with some four hundred soldiers and a retinue of *caballeros* who had volunteered to fight the Pechelingues.[22]

---

[21] *Ibid.*, 82-85; 101-103.
[22] *Ibid.*, 109. Letter from viceroy, October 28, 1615, in *México* 28, AGI. Portillo, *Descubrimientos,* 454.

Meanwhile Speilbergen's fleet was battered in a hurricane off Guatemala and proceeded slowly up the coast in search of provisions, which had become very scarce. The total strength had been reduced to about 650 men, most of them suffering from scurvy. Longboats were sent in to examine the coast, and one or two of them arrived on October 2 at the port of Guatulco, which still had a small settlement. Here they were hailed from the shore and promised provisions, but the crew did not wish to risk landing in such small force. Adverse winds prevented the fleet from entering Guatulco and probably saved that unfortunate port from another sacking.[23]

The morning of October 11, one of those almost windless days common in the midst of the hurricane season, found the Dutch fleet becalmed just outside the entrance to Acapulco. The ships edged their way into the harbor and anchored boldly before the improvised fort shortly after noon. The Spaniards had ample opportunity to test their cannon, firing about ten shot with such poor effect that no damage whatever was done. Speilbergen, whose desperate need of victuals had determined him to destroy the town if it became necessary,

---

[23] Speilbergen, *op. cit.*, 105. The name of Guatulco is not mentioned in Speilbergen's journal, but the place is described as "a very convenient bay . . . where we could anchor quite comfortably." There is no other such port for many miles in either direction. Furthermore the viceroy in his letter of October 28 (*México* 28, AGI) mentions that two *"vajeles"* had entered Guatulco.

held his fire and sent off a launch with a white flag, which was met by a boatload of Spanish officials. A truce was declared, and two of the Spaniards went aboard the flagship, where they were hospitably received by the admiral. These men, Pedro Alvarez and Francisco Menéndez, spoke Dutch, having served with the Spanish forces in the Netherlands some years past. Speilbergen broached to them his desire to take on provisions in exchange for the Spanish prisoners he had brought from Peru, and the two officers promised to do what they could to carry out such an arrangement. They returned ashore, and the Dutch towed their ships closer to the town and dropped anchor directly under the gun emplacements, where they must have spent an unpleasant night.[24]

The following day an impression that the Spaniards were about to make an unfriendly move caused Speilbergen to move out and train his guns on the shore batteries, but the tension was relaxed when Menéndez and Alvarez came back aboard the flagship and offered to remain as hostages. The result of their parley was an agreement to continue the truce while the fleet was provisioned, at the end of which time the Dutch would release their prisoners and leave.[25]

For a week Acapulco was the scene of a rare social mingling between the Dutch and Spanish

---

[24] Speilbergen, *op. cit.*, 106-107. *México* 28, AGI, *loc. cit.*
[25] *Ibid.*

officers, each side observing the strictest ceremony and punctilio. Many "captains and cavallieros" visited the pirate ships, where they were treated to ample Dutch hospitality and allowed to examine the armament and fittings. On the fifteenth, Speilbergen received a visit from Fernández de Córdoba, the Spanish commander. For such a distinguished guest the Dutch admiral had his troops drawn up in full parade uniform with muskets and swords. At the same time, to guarantee the safety of Fernández, Speilbergen's young son went ashore and spent the day with the *alcalde mayor,* by whom he was "very honourably received and entertained." [26]

Meanwhile the Dutch sailors, working shoulder-to-shoulder with the citizenry of Acapulco, were busy bringing out to their ships casks of fresh water, wood for the cooking fires, and a good supply of food, principally meat and fowls, vegetables, oranges, and lemons. On October 16, while provisions were still being brought out, the Dutch set ashore their twenty Spanish prisoners. The next day, having received all the supplies agreed on, the pirates took leave of their new friends with many expressions of mutual esteem. Early in the morning of October 18, the Dutch squadron weighed anchor and sailed out of Acapulco with a good breeze.[27]

---

[26] Speilbergen, *op. cit.,* 108.
[27] *Ibid. México* 28, AGI, *loc. cit.*

The friendly atmosphere of the truce at Acapulco was in sharp contrast with Speilbergen's
subsequent adventures in New Spain. While com-
pliments were being exchanged at the port, the
viceroy ordered every available ship on the coast
to proceed to Cedros Island in order to alert and
protect the Manila galleons which were soon expected. Guessing that the pirates might call there,
the viceroy sent Sebastián Vizcaíno with two hundred soldiers to protect the ports of Navidad and
Salagua. Independently the governor of Nueva
Vizcaya sent down another body of troops to the
coast of Sinaloa under Bartolomé Juárez de
Villalva, also to alert the galleons and prevent
enemy landings.[28]

After leaving Acapulco, the Dutch squadron
was becalmed for a week off Zacatula. On the
morning of October 26 they came up on a rather
large ship at anchor near the shore, which was
promptly boarded in the face of a few harquebus
shot and taken as a prize. She was the pearler "San
Francisco," a new, well-built ship of two hundred
tons commanded by Nicolás de Cardona, bound
from California to Acapulco. Cardona and others
of his crew escaped by swimming to shore, but the
Dutch took eleven prisoners, including two Franciscan priests, *sargento mayor* Pedro Alvarez de
Rosales, and a pilot who had had experience in the
Manila trade. Cardona claims that he was robbed

28 *México* 28, AGI, *loc. cit.* Portillo, *Descubrimientos,* 455.

of some pearls, but this is denied by Speilbergen. The latter comments that the prize "seemed to have been fitted out for war rather than for fishing," as she carried four cannon, two mortars, and other small arms and munitions. The Dutch renamed her "Perel" ("Pearl") and took her, together with the pilot and one of the priests, all the way to the East Indies.[29]

His prisoners, perhaps with malice aforethought, told Speilbergen that he could obtain provisions at Salagua. Accordingly the Dutch squadron arrived there in the evening of November 10, and sent ashore two boats with heavily armed crews. It would seem that Vizcaíno's two hundred soldiers, having arrived two days before and at the moment hiding nearby in the woods, had carelessly left a great number of bootprints on the beach. This alerted the pirates, who immediately returned to their ships. Before nightfall Speilbergen set ashore the prisoner Alvarez with a letter stating his peaceful intentions and his desire to secure a few supplies.[30]

Early the following morning seven boats pulled away from the Dutch ships and landed with about two hundred men.[31] To the dismay of Vizcaíno,

---

[29] Speilbergen, *op. cit.*, 109-110. Letter from Vizcaíno, November 12, 1615, in *México* 28, AGI. Portillo, *op. cit.*, 455.

[30] Speilbergen, *op. cit.*, 111. The Dutch could not have needed more supplies very badly. They must have been lingering in hope of meeting the galleons.

[31] Vizcaíno estimated the Dutch strength at 400. Letter, November 12, 1615, in *México* 28, AGI.

who had spent all night in a well-prepared ambush along the trail, the pirates started inland along another route. The Spaniards re-grouped and attacked, and a battle ensued which lasted, according to Vizcaíno, from 8 a.m. until 2 p.m., at which time both sides ran out of powder and retired. When the Dutch returned with more ammunition the Spaniards fled to the woods.[32]

According to Speilbergen, only two of his men were killed and six or seven injured in this engagement, while the Spaniards had "many" dead and wounded. Vizcaíno in his report told a somewhat different story: great enemy losses, seven dead pirates left on the beach, and seven prisoners taken. As of possible interest to the viceroy, Vizcaíno was sending with his letter the ears of a pirate. He admitted to four Spaniards killed and three injured. His victory would have been more complete, said Vizcaíno, but his men were inexperienced and the pirates had modern muskets, while the Spaniards had only ancient harquebuses and *escopetas de piedra* (flintlocks) which misfired most of the time. Vizcaíno described his "pechelingas" prisoners as "youths and very gentle men, some of them Irish, with great forelocks and ear-

---

[32] *México* 28, AGI, *loc. cit.* Speilbergen, *op. cit.,* 111. Speilbergen makes light of this skirmish and implies that it lasted only a short time. It is hard to believe that it continued for six hours; within that time the Dutch would have had reinforcements. Perhaps Vizcaíno exaggerated a bit in his report to the viceroy. Speilbergen's account has the enemy flee before his men, while Vizcaíno admits he retired when the Dutch returned with more ammunition. See illustration at page 125.

rings." All the prisoners declared that they were good Catholics who had been lured aboard Speilbergen's ships under the illusion that they were going on a peaceful trading voyage.[33]

Immediately after the battle at Salagua, Speilbergen moved his ships around to the adjoining harbor of Santiago. On November 15-16 the squadron sailed up the coast and entered the port of Navidad, or more likely what is now Tenacatita, where the admiral himself went ashore with a strong force. The place was deserted, Vizcaíno and his men having already passed through bound northward. The Pechelingues spent five days in this quiet and beautiful bay, resting and swimming in its warm, clear waters, gathering wood and filling their water casks from a little river. One of the Franciscan prisoners was sent inland to an Indian village to negotiate for supplies, and returned with some chickens and fresh fruit.[34]

On November 20 the Dutch squadron sailed out of Navidad and ran up the coast to Cape Corrientes. Speilbergen called a broad council meeting, in which there was considerable difference of opinion. Some wanted to wait for the Manila

---

[33] *Ibid.* The prisoners were later sent to Spain: Letter from viceroy, May 25, 1616, in *México* 28, AGI.

[34] Speilbergen, *op. cit.,* 111-112. There is some doubt whether the Dutch called at Navidad or at the nearby bay of Tenacatita. Navidad is clearly identified in a log of 1602, at which time the shipyard was still in existence (Portillo, *Descubrimientos,* 339). Speilbergen does not mention the shipyard, and his map of "Natividaet" (page 125) looks more like Tenacatita than Navidad.

galleons at San Lucas, while others reasoned that this would result in too long a delay, and that in any case the galleons would have been warned to stand well out to sea, making their capture very unlikely. Finally it was decided to waste no more time in Mexican waters, and on December 2, 1615, the fleet left Cape Corrientes and headed southwestward across the Pacific. The decision was a fortunate one for the Spaniards, as only a few days afterward the first of two Manila galleons passed the cape bound for Acapulco.[35]

Seven months later Speilbergen reached Holland by way of the East Indies, having accomplished nearly everything he had set out to do. He made no other voyages of importance, and died a poor man in 1620.

Within a month after the departure of Speilbergen, construction began on the castle of San Diego de Acapulco. The viceroy planned to raise funds for this project by levying a special tax of two per cent on all merchandise arriving in the port for the next six years. He also suggested the maintenance of a permanent fleet of four warships to patrol the coast from the Straits of Magellan to Cape San Lucas and escort the treasure galleons. The king agreed to the construction of a fort (by

[35] Speilbergen, op. cit., 112-113. Sluiter MS., 179. Two galleons crossed that year, reaching Acapulco on December 24, 1615, and January 1, 1616: México 28, AGI.

that time it was almost finished), but the idea of a defense fleet was disapproved because of the expense. Instead, steps were taken to reduce the volume of maritime traffic between Peru and Mexico. In a cédula of 1620 the king limited trade between the two viceroyalties to a single ship yearly, and repeated the old order forbidding the sale of Chinese goods in Peru. The contraband trade in these goods, however, continued on a large scale. In February, 1616, a meeting was held in Mexico City with the commanders of the Manila ships to discuss changing the route of these vessels to make their capture more difficult. It was decided that they should keep one hundred leagues off California and New Spain on the return voyage, approaching Acapulco from the sea rather than along the coast. This order was not entirely carried out, although Cape San Lucas was given a wide berth for the next few years.[36]

While there was a lull in enemy activities, the danger was by no means past. The Dutchman Jacob le Maire, in 1616, discovered a new means of entry into the Pacific south of Tierra del Fuego, through the strait which still bears his name. In 1620 there was a report of twelve enemy ships off Peru, which were supposed to be heading toward Panamá. Nothing more is known of this phantom squadron except that it did not appear anywhere

---

[36] Letters from viceroy, October 28, 1615; January 25, February 26, and May 25, 1616; in *México* 28, AGI. Borah, *Colonial Trade*, 127.

else.[37] Then in 1621 the so-called truce between Holland and Spain came to an end, and the Dutch made ready the most powerful enemy fleet ever to appear on the Mexican west coast.

Prince Mauritius of Nassau and the States General of Holland, in dispatching to the Pacific what was known as the Nassau Fleet, had more in mind than contraband trade and the sacking of Spanish ports and ships.[38] For the first time it was proposed to challenge Spanish sovereignty on the mainland of South America. Included in the fleet's instructions was a paragraph providing for the establishment of a Dutch military and trading colony in Peru or Chile. This was to be done by combining forces with the Indians, who it was assumed could easily be induced to turn against their Spanish masters. The idea was not without possibilities, since the fierce Araucanians had been fighting the Spaniards with success for many years. The admiral put in charge of this ambitious venture was Jacob l'Heremite. Unfortunately for the plans of the Dutch, l'Heremite died on the coast of Peru and the command devolved upon the young vice-admiral, Hugo Schapenham. Altogether the

[37] Portillo, *Descubrimientos*, 456.

[38] The main source is *Journael van de Nassausche Vloot* (Amsterdam, 1626), used by Burney, *Chronological History*, III, pp. 2-32. See also Adolph Decker's journal, found in [Callander], *Terra Australis Cognita*, II, pp. 287-327.

fleet consisted of ten ships and a *jacht,* with a total
of 292 guns and 1,637 men, six hundred of whom
were soldiers. The complements were composed
almost entirely of Dutchmen with a few English
and French. Pertinent data of the various ships
are given in the adjoining table.[39]

Ship	*Tons*	*Men*	*Guns*
Amsterdam (admiral) .	800	237	42
Delft (vice-admiral) . .	800	242	40
Orangien	700	216	40
Hollandia	600	182	30
Eendracht	600	170	32
Arend	400	144	28
Mauritius	360	169	32
David	360	99	16
Griffioen	320	78	14
Verwachting	260	80	14
Windhond *(jacht)* . . .	60	20	4

This formidable squadron sailed from Holland
at the end of April, 1623. A good deal of time was
spent on the west coast of Africa before they
crossed the south Atlantic and entered the Pacific,
through the strait recently discovered by le Maire
and around Cape Horn, in February, 1624. The
inevitable bad weather caused the squadron to be
divided, but all eleven ships met at Juan Fernández
Island in April.

The enemy arrived off Callao on May 8, just
five days after the forewarned viceroy had sent off
for Panamá a treasure fleet carrying two years'

---

[39] Callander, *op. cit.,* II, p. 287. Burney, *op. cit.,* III, p. 3.

BATTLE BETWEEN THE SPANIARDS AND PECHELINGUES AT SALAGUA

From a contemporary Dutch engraving.

accumulation of silver.[40] Rather than pursue this rich quarry the Dutch fell into a state of indecision and confusion which can be charitably attributed to the loss of their commander. An ill-managed attack on Callao was repulsed by the Spaniards, although the enemy destroyed a number of merchant vessels in the port.[41] At this point the fleet's council formally installed Hugo Schapenham as admiral. Among his men there seems to have been a wide difference of opinion regarding Schapenham's character. He was described by a captain of marines as "a man of sweet disposition," [42] while a Dutch gunner captured by the Spaniards referred to him as "a haughty young man, and very cruel." [43] We can infer from subsequent events that he was plagued by indecision and by the inability to control his subordinates. His youth and lack of experience made him an unfortunate choice for the command of such a large enterprise.

The Nassau Fleet spent over four months on the coast of Peru, accomplishing little other than the destruction of Guayaquil and the acquiring of an evil reputation for inhuman treatment of Spanish prisoners.[44] Schapenham sailed from the Gulf of

---

[40] Fernández Duro, *Armada Española*, IV, pp. 35-36.

[41] Burney, *op. cit.*, III, p. 20. Bancroft, *New Pacific*, 484.

[42] Callander, *op. cit.*, II, p. 287.

[43] Burney, *op. cit.*, III, p. 22.

[44] *Ibid.*, III, pp. 24, 27. Fernández Duro, *op. cit.*, IV, p. 38. Twenty-one Spanish prisoners were hanged at Callao because the viceroy refused to pay ransom or turn over Dutch deserters. Seventeen prisoners taken at Guayaquil were thrown overboard miles from shore.

Guayaquil in mid-September, 1624, arriving on the coast of New Spain on October 20. At this time his fleet was intact and still had more than thirteen hundred men.

Eight days later the Dutch entered the harbor of Acapulco and dropped anchor within sight of the new fort. Emulating his illustrious predecessor Speilbergen, Schapenham sent a message to the *castellano* proposing a truce. He was in need of supplies which he was willing to accept in return for the few Spanish prisoners that had survived. To the chagrin of the Dutch the *castellano* offered only a money ransom, refused to victual the enemy, and would not even exchange hostages. Schapenham had sufficient cannon and men to destroy Acapulco, but he hesitated to attempt it. With one eye on the bristling guns of the castle the admiral reasoned, quite correctly, that the countryside was probably barren of provisions and there would be little in the way of booty until the Manila galleon came in. Consequently, on November 1 the great Nassau Fleet hoisted sail and ignominiously slunk out of the harbor, followed by a few shot from the proud fortress of San Diego. Burney comments, "Thus cheaply were the Spaniards freed from the most formidable armament that ever at any time before or since threatened their possessions in the South Sea." [45]

---

[45] Burney, *op. cit.*, III, pp. 30-32. Callander, *op. cit.*, II, pp. 325-326. Cavo, *Historia de México*, 294, gives the false impression that the Nassau Fleet took Acapulco without resistance.

With their hasty departure the Dutch had not even been able to replenish their dwindling water supply. The squadron separated off Acapulco, some of the ships beating up northwest to wait for the galleon, others standing outside the harbor they had just left. On November 3 and succeeding days a few boatloads of men went into Puerto Marqués, adjacent to Acapulco, and managed to fill some of their water casks before they were driven off by the Spaniards with a loss of four men. Two of the ships then succeeded in finding a deserted watering place a short distance up the coast. With great difficulty, because of the heavy surf, they got off with their casks just before a large party of Spaniards appeared.[46]

Schapenham's men, ravaged with scurvy and disgusted with the irresolute behavior of their commander, which they ascribed to cowardice, were now thoroughly demoralized. At least thirty of them, perhaps more, preferred taking their chances with the enemy and deserted. The fleet was reunited off Zihuatanejo in mid-November, and on the twenty-ninth of that month the Dutch gave up their wait for the Manila ship and left the coast of Mexico to cross the Pacific. Subsequently the squadron was disbanded in the Moluccas. Schapenham died, off the island of Java, toward the end of 1625.[47]

---

[46] *Ibid.*

[47] Burney, *op. cit.*, III, p. 32. Callander, *op. cit.*, II, p. 327.

The Dutch had placed great expectations and invested a large amount of money in the cruise of the Nassau squadron. After its dismal failure they confined hostile activities to the Atlantic side of America for several years, and succeeded in capturing the Mexican silver fleet in 1628. The great treasure galleons of the Pacific were left undisturbed for a time. In 1631 the king ordered a stop to the annual sailing of the only legal trading ship between New Spain and Peru, which meant that the still considerable quantities of silver and contraband merchandise would henceforth move between the two viceroyalties without any semblance of royal protection.[48] After Schapenham's visit the viceroy of Peru strengthened Callao's defenses and maintained two strongly-armed galleons, a smaller ship, and a number of armed galleys to protect the port and convoy the silver shipments to Panamá.[49] In New Spain the viceroy had certain repairs and improvements made to the Castle of San Diego in Acapulco, which after 1616 was the only seaport legally open to commerce on the Mexican west coast.[50]

In the fall of 1632 New Spain was again alerted to the danger of pirates. News arrived from Peru that five enemy ships had come into the South Sea around Cape Horn.[51] Then three ships, thought to

---

[48] Borah, *Colonial Trade,* 127.
[49] Vázquez Espinosa, *Compendio,* 425.
[50] Letter from viceroy, May 2, 1632, in *México* 31, AGI.
[51] Fernández Duro, *op. cit.,* IV, p. 342.

be Dutch Pechelingues, were seen near a port in the *audiencia* of Guadalajara. The largest was described as being of about three hundred tons, the others one hundred tons each. The viceroy sent out several vessels to warn the Manila galleons off Lower California, and troops were again mobilized, but the alarm seems to have been a false one.[52] Perhaps the ships seen belonged to some clandestine pearling expedition.

The last serious effort of the Dutch to harass the Spaniards in the Pacific was the expedition of Hendrick Brouwer. The Dutch West India Company, of which Brouwer was a director, decided to make another attempt to establish a trading colony in Chile. A squadron of three ships left Holland in November, 1642, and joined by other vessels in Brazil the fleet rounded Cape Horn and arrived off Chiloe Island in May, 1643. Brouwer died a few months later, but his men stayed on at Valdivia, built a fort there, and engaged in hostilities with the Spaniards.[53]

When this news reached Mexico early in December, 1643, there was not a single ship in Acapulco to defend the coast or serve as escort for the Manila galleons. This duty was entrusted to Don Pedro Porter Casanate, who had a small armed vessel at the mouth of Río Grande de Santiago which he planned to use for an exploration of

[52] *Patronato Real* 30, *ramo* 4; letter from viceroy, November 20, 1632, in *México* 31, AGI.
[53] Burney, *Chronological History*, III, pp. 113-145.

Lower California. Porter's ship crossed the gulf
to San Lucas, where she remained a month waiting
for the galleon.[54] The latter had already sailed by
and reached Acapulco without incident.[55]

Meanwhile, in their bleak settlement far to the
south, the Dutch had consumed their provisions
and found the Indians disinclined to help them
conquer Chile from the Spaniards. They sailed
from Valdivia at the end of October, 1643, returning to the Atlantic.[56]

Another report of enemy ships in the Pacific
reached Mexico City in November, 1649. The
castellano of Acapulco sent an urgent message
asking for additional soldiers to defend the port
against five large ships which had made their
appearance on the coast. They were supposed to be
manned by certain Portuguese who had committed
atrocities in Buenos Aires, stolen the ships, and
sailed into the Pacific on a pirate cruise. Once
again troops hurried down to the coast, warnings
were sent to all seaports, and Porter Casanate was
dispatched to warn the China ship. And once again
the phantom pirate ships vanished into the air.[57]

The era of the Pechelingues formally came to an
end with the Peace of Westphalia in 1649. Dutch
pirates still infested the Caribbean, but they did
not return to the Pacific except in the guise of
innocent traders many years later.

[54] *Colección de Documentos Inéditos*, IX, pp. 5-18.
[55] Portillo, *Descubrimientos*, 488.
[56] Burney, *op. cit.*, III, pp. 142-144.
[57] Guijo, *Diario*, I, pp. 71-72. Portillo, *op. cit.*, 521.

IV
The Buccaneers

The Buccaneers

The various enemy incursions into the Spanish Pacific through the year 1643 were for the most part affairs of state, undertaken in time of war or at least sponsored in some way by the governments of England and Holland for the purpose of increasing their markets, strengthening their prestige, or generally furthering their national interests. We now come to a somewhat different sort of enemy, one to whom the term "pirate" can be applied without hesitation. The buccaneers who cruised the Caribbean were at first tolerated and to some extent encouraged by the English, French, and Dutch governments for the harm they did to their common enemy, Spain. Occasionally they even carried commissions from some recognized authority, but only as a formality and a convenience. They were a hardy and cruel breed of independent sea robbers, interested primarily in acquiring booty to gratify their own ephemeral pleasures. To achieve this end they tortured, raped, and committed every sort of atrocity. The chronicler of the Sawkins-Sharp expedition cynically admits, "'twas Gold was the bait that tempted a Pack of merry Boys of us . . . being all Souldiers of fortune, to list our selves in the service of one of the Rich West Indian Monarchs, the Emperour of *Darien*."[1] The latter was a naked Indian chief, and in no sense commanded the allegiance of the pirates but merely furnished an excuse for their forays.

These pirates preferred to band together with others of their own country and language, but sometimes their crews were a mixture of French, English, Dutch, and other nationalities, and not infrequently pirate gangs of one nation would join forces with those of another for a particular raid or cruise. There was little discipline in their ships. Desertions and mutinies were common, and when a captain lost favor with his men he was simply "turned out," and a new leader elected by majority vote. Silver and gold stolen in the buccaneer raids were usually divided among the men according to a fixed system of shares, while individual pirates could keep jewelry and other personally acquired booty.[2]

In the 1640s the buccaneers, in alliance with the Mosquito and other Indian tribes, gained control of those vast sections of the east coast of Central America which had been left unconquered by the Spaniards. Inevitably their greed was aroused by the flourishing Spanish settlements to the west. As

---

[1] Ayres, *Voyages and adventures*, 1.

[2] For details of buccaneer life and organization, see Esquemeling, *Buccaneers of America*.

early as 1643 there is a report of a pirate raid
inland to the town of Matagalpa, in west central
Nicaragua.[3] In 1654 a large number of pirates
ascended the Segovia or Coco River from Cape
Gracias á Dios, hauling their canoes around the
rapids, and sacked the mining town of Nueva
Segovia.[4] A pirate captain named Mansvelt is said
to have taken a small band across the isthmus, captured a vessel, and cruised for a short while on the
west coast of Nicaragua, probably about 1660. He
soon returned to the Caribbean because he was
unable to accomplish anything with such a small
force.[5]

The Desaguadero of Lake Nicaragua (San Juan
River) was a relatively easy means of transit between the two seas and had been used as such by
the Spaniards for many years. When the buccaneers
closed this natural canal to commerce, and furthermore began to use it themselves, the authorities of
Nicaragua built a fortress at San Carlos, at the
eastern outlet of the lake. A pirate expedition
seems to have made its way up the river in 1665,
captured the fort, and continued through Lake
Nicaragua to Granada and beyond to León and
Realejo on the Pacific, doing some damage to those
places. One account says that the buccaneers, pur-

[3] *Colección de libros y documentos,* VIII, p. xxi.
[4] Bancroft, *Central America,* II, p. 454. Dampier, *New Voyage,* 95.
[5] Masefield, *Spanish Main,* 133. Esquemeling, *Buccaneers of America,* 74.

sued by an army of Spaniards, got back to the Caribbean with 50,000 pesos in loot.[6]

The following year, 1666, Captain Mansvelt and a new arrival, Henry Morgan, with seven or eight hundred pirates, attempted to invade Costa Rica. They were met by a Spanish force at Turrialba and were obliged to retreat to the Caribbean. Morgan returned to capture Porto Belo, which he held for a while in the summer of 1668.[7]

Soon the buccaneers were to make their presence painfully felt in the Pacific. But to keep the chronological order straight we must digress to report on another false alarm. Captain John Narbrough was sent out by the British admiralty in 1669, with two ships and a hundred men, on a voyage of trade and discovery. He was ordered to explore the west coast of America, and was specifically directed to avoid hostilities with the Spaniards. He went through the Straits of Magellan and arrived off Valdivia, in southern Chile, in December, 1670. News of another enemy was sent up the coast, reaching Mexico in May of the following year

[6] *Colección de libros y documentos*, VIII, p. xxi. Esquemeling, *Buccaneers of America*, 74 ff. Bancroft, *Central America*, II, p. 441. The first source attributes this raid to a party led by Juan Davis, who "tried to take Granada" in June, 1665; it speaks of a second invasion led by Gallardillo, who captured the fort in 1670. Esquemeling, without mentioning the date, tells of John Davis's raid with eighty men in three canoes, when the "town of Nicaragua" (modern Rivas?) was sacked. Bancroft says the 1665 raid was led by Gallardillo who captured and burned Granada and also sacked Realejo.

[7] Peralta, *Costa-Rica y Colombia*, 69. Bancroft, *Central America*, II, p. 460.

and causing the usual commotion. Narbrough, his
innocent plans thwarted when the Spaniards captured some of his men, spent only a week in Chile
before returning to the Atlantic.[8]

Henry Morgan, born of honest Welsh parents
about 1635, was probably the most unsavory pirate
to reach the shores of the Pacific. In his youth he
had fallen into the hands of the Spaniards, and his
mistreatment by them served as a motive for the
fierce revenge he later exacted. In 1670 he conceived the idea of crossing the isthmus and sacking
the city of Panamá. To carry out this ambitious
project, disguised as a patriotic venture to forestall
a proposed Spanish attack on Jamaica, Morgan
sent out a call for volunteers which was answered,
according to Masefield, by "all the ruffians of the
Indies." [9] First securing, after a bloody attack, the
Atlantic fortress of San Lorenzo at the mouth of
the Chagres, some fourteen hundred buccaneers
began the arduous trip across the isthmus in mid-
January, 1671. The Spaniards, with ample warning, had prepared numerous ambushes and destroyed everything edible along the route. Consequently the pirates arrived before Panamá City in
a particularly ugly mood.
    Panamá at this time may well have been the

---

[8] Burney, *Chronological History*, III, pp. 316-371. Letter from viceroy, May 25, 1671, in *México* 45, AGI.
[9] Masefield, *Spanish Main*, 168.

richest center of commerce in America. The city
had fifteen or twenty thousand inhabitants, including slaves and mulattoes. We have mentioned that
old Panamá, while it had a small fort facing the
sea, normally had no provision whatever for
defense from the land. Breastworks were now
hastily erected and a few guns were moved around
to cover the main entrance to the city, but Morgan
avoided them by approaching from a different
quarter. On January 29 the pirates were met outside the city by a large force commanded by Don
Juan Pérez de Guzmán, president of the *audiencia*.
The total Spanish strength was about two thousand
men, most of them Negro militia and including
two hundred cavalry. In a vicious two-hour battle
Morgan's men routed the enemy, killing some four
hundred Spaniards. Pirate losses were about two
hundred dead. A few hours later, after considerable fighting in the streets, the buccaneers were in
possession of the city.[10]

Morgan and his band remained over a month in
Panamá, looting and applying the most fiendish
tortures to their prisoners in order to find more
gold. Most of the wooden houses were destroyed
by fire. A Captain Searles was sent out in a captured vessel and took four more prizes in the gulf
and around Taboga Island. Other pirate crews
then went out in the prizes and rummaged the

[10] *Ibid.*, 197-202. Esquemeling, *op. cit.*, 218-220. Ayres, *Voyages and
adventures*, 135-141, 145-156.

Pearl Islands and nearby coastal settlements. Some of the buccaneers made plans to stay and cruise in the Pacific, but when Morgan heard of it he had all the vessels burned or dismantled and their cannon spiked.[11]

On March 6, 1671, the pirates left Panamá taking with them six hundred still unransomed prisoners and a good amount of loot – estimates range from 150,000 to 750,000 pesos. Morgan reached the Caribbean on March 19 and secretly embarked with most of the booty, leaving his infuriated fellow pirates on the shore.[12] Later he became lieutenant-governor of Jamaica, was knighted, and did much to suppress piracy. He died in 1688.

Sometime in late 1671 or early 1672 a flotilla of strange ships appeared on the west coast of South America. It would seem that they were traders out of Amsterdam, sent by a company of Dutch and English merchants who had somehow contrived to get from the Spaniards special permission to sell their goods in the American colonies.[13] We know little about this most unusual expedition, and Spanish reports on the size and composition of

---

[11] Masefield, *op. cit.*, 202-209. Ayres, *op. cit.*, 142.

[12] Masefield, *op. cit.*, 210-217. Ayres, *op. cit.*, 143. The latter account, perhaps written by Morgan, says the treasure amounted to only £30,000 which was fairly divided among the pirates.

[13] Burney, *Chronological History*, III, p. 383.

the fleet are conflicting.[14] They were not pirates, but they might as well have been for all the panic and confusion they caused in New Spain.

Most of the cargo of these vessels was sold advantageously at Guayaquil and Realejo.[15] They then apparently proceeded up the coast toward Acapulco. The viceroy first heard about them when "five pirate ships" were reported to be anchored off Tulancingo (near Jamiltepec) on July 13, 1672.[16] The *castellano* of Acapulco, who had retired to Cuernavaca for the hot season, suddenly became too ill to travel down to the port.[17] Troops were immediately dispatched to Acapulco under the command of Diego Centeno, "Lieutenant General of All the South Sea Coasts." A few days later, on the twenty-third, six ships were seen going by Acapulco bound for the north. In August they appeared off Motines province,[18] and in September "fourteen English ships" entered the Bay of Salagua.[19] As the enemy seemed to be headed toward their jurisdiction, the *audiencia* of Guadalajara appointed one of their *oidores*, Don Gerónimo de Luna, to be general of a second army which proceeded to the coast to repel the invasion.[20]

---

[14] Burney says there was only a 400-ton ship and an 80-ton bilander. Mexican estimates range from five to fourteen ships, but there is no certainty that they are referring to the same expedition.

[15] Burney, *loc. cit.*

[16] Letter from Antonio Dávila, July 14, 1672, in *México* 46, AGI.

[17] Letter from viceroy, July 23, 1672, in *México* 46, AGI.

[18] *Idem*, October 22, 1672, *ibid.*

[19] Robles, *Diario*, I, p. 122.

[20] *Ibid.*

All cattle were ordered to be moved twenty leagues inland. The viceroy was so interested in getting information about these "pirates" that he offered a reward for taking the first enemy prisoner: if the captor were a slave he was to be given his freedom, if a free man he would receive three hundred pesos.[21] On October 4 the enemy vessels, now seven in number, came in to a harbor called Tiacapan, south of Mazatlán, and the pirates were reported to have stolen some cattle.[22] Then suddenly the strange ships disappeared as mysteriously as they had arrived. In his final report the viceroy seems to be rather skeptical of the whole business.[23] The traders, if such they were, are said to have returned to Holland after a most prosperous voyage.[24]

In the years 1674-1676 at least two squadrons of non-Spanish ships made their appearance in the Pacific, and two different bands of buccaneers invaded Central America.

Antonio de la Roche, a London-born merchant of French ancestry, laded two vessels at Hamburg with trading goods and sailed around Cape Horn in September, 1674. Officially the exclusive Spanish trade policy had not changed, but Spain had

---

[21] Letter from viceroy, July 28, 1672, in *México* 46, AGI.

[22] *Idem*, October 22, 1672, *ibid*. Robles, *Diario*, I, p. 122, confusingly states that fourteen ships called at Salagua, "near the mining town of Copala in the diocese of Guadiana." Copala was far north of Salagua, near Mazatlán.

[23] Letter of October 22, 1672, in *México* 46, AGI.

[24] Burney, *op. cit.*, III, p. 383.

never been able to satisfy her colonies' demands for European goods, and consequently contraband trade had assumed large proportions. De la Roche met with no opposition in disposing of his cargo in Peru, and returned by the same route to Europe.[25] In January, 1676, a report of "many enemy ships in the Straits of Magellan" reached Mexico.[26] We can guess that these were the vessels of de la Roche.

Thomas Peche was an English pirate who cruised for some years in the Caribbean before undertaking a remarkable voyage in the years 1673-1677. He sailed from England with three vessels, a flagship of 500 tons and forty-four guns, and two frigates of 150 tons and eighteen guns each. Peche rounded Cape Horn and crossed the South Pacific to the Moluccas, captured a Spanish ship in the Philippines, and then followed the track of the Manila galleons across the northern Pacific with the intention of returning to England through the Straits of Anian. We are told that he was prevented by contrary winds and currents from entering that mythical passage.[27] Peche seems to have visited briefly the west coast of New Spain toward the end of 1675 or early in 1676, calling at Guatulco.[28] He reached England by way of the Straits of Magellan the following year.

---

[25] *Ibid.*, III, pp. 395-404.

[26] Robles, *Diario*, I, p. 191.

[27] Burney, *op. cit.*, III, pp. 393-394.

[28] Robles, *op. cit.*, I, p. 193. On January 28, 1676, news reached Mexico City from Guatulco that two "enemy" ships had arrived there, but it was thought they might be Peruvian contraband vessels.

A French pirate by the name of Lessone, alias La Sound, is said to have marched overland with one hundred twenty men, in 1675, to the settlement of Chepó east of Panamá City, before being driven back by the Spaniards.[29] The following year another and considerably larger body of buccaneers, perhaps eight hundred men including Indian allies, went up the Segovia River from Cape Gracias a Dios. For the second time the old mining settlement of Nueva Segovia was pillaged, on May 12, 1676. This pirate band then returned to the Caribbean and on June 30 invaded the valley of Matina to the south. Their intention was to drive the Spaniards out of Costa Rica in order to have a convenient base for their activities in the South Sea. However the governor of Costa Rica, Don Juan Francisco Sáenz, defeated the buccaneers in a nineteen-day campaign in which he claimed to have killed more than two hundred of them.[30]

It was now clear to the Spaniards that Morgan's successful raid on Panamá had encouraged others to follow in his wake. The Caribbean was becoming overcrowded with buccaneers and it was time for the Pacific to get its share of the scourge. There were several overland routes which might be followed to get from the Atlantic side of Central America to the Pacific. The Segovia River could be ascended in canoes for several hundred miles

[29] Dampier, *New Voyage*, 128-130.
[30] Peralta, *Costa-Rica y Colombia*, 69-71.

through friendly or neutral Indian country, but before reaching its headwaters the pirates would be surrounded by aroused and reinforced Spaniards. The same problem existed with the Nicaragua waterway, which now had several strong forts on the Desaguadero. Costa Rica and Veragua were even more difficult because of the high mountains which had to be crossed, and the silver route from Porto Belo to Panamá was very strongly guarded after Morgan's raid. However, a few miles east of Panamá the Spanish settlements came to an end, and there was a stretch of wild country inhabited by Indians who were hostile to the Spaniards. Here the mountains were relatively low, and faint Indian trails threaded the swamps and the luxuriant jungle. This route was to become an inter-oceanic highway for the buccaneers.

In April, 1680, a major buccaneer invasion of the Pacific took place.[31] Seven pirate ships, all English, rendezvoused at Golden Island (one of the Sasardí group) on the north coast of Panamá. These buccaneers had recently got away from Porto Belo with a large amount of Spanish gold. When the Indians told them of a rich new mining camp at Santa María, directly across the isthmus,

[31] The expedition of Sawkins, Sharp, *et al.*, is described in detail by Ringrose (in Esquemeling, *Buccaneers of America,* 285 ff) and Ayres, *Voyages and adventures,* 1-84. Masefield, *Spanish Main,* 233-289, gives an admirable synthesis of these sources. The account given here is taken from Masefield except where otherwise indicated.

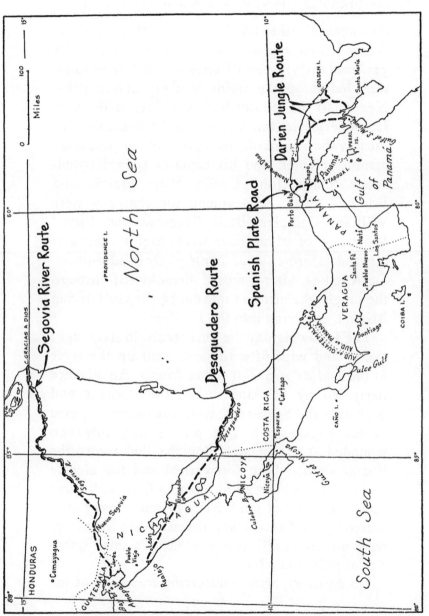

PIRATE TRAILS ACROSS CENTRAL AMERICA

they determined to try their luck in that direction. A small force remained to guard the ships, while 331 men carrying small arms and a few supplies were led across the divide by their Indian allies. Nearly all the pirates had new French muskets, far superior to the antiquated harquebuses still used by the Spaniards. Richard Sawkins was commander-in-chief, and his captains were Bartholomew Sharp, John Coxon, Peter Harris, and Edmund Cook. Also among the company were William Dampier, Basil Ringrose, and Lionel Wafer, all of whom later wrote highly entertaining and informative accounts of their adventures. On April 24, after a record nine-day trip through the jungle, the pirates came out on the Gulf of San Miguel, emptying into the Pacific.

The following day the buccaneers, in sixty-eight canoes and with fifty Indians, went up the river to the *real de minas* of Santa María. An advance party led by Sawkins rushed the stockade and overcame the Spaniards, who lost twenty-six men in the engagement. The pirates had only two wounded. Unfortunately for the buccaneers the Spaniards had been forewarned and the *alcalde mayor* was on his way to Panamá City with three hundredweight of gold. Fifty prisoners were massacred by the Indians, and the surviving Spaniards were tortured until they yielded up a small quantity of gold and silver.

On April 27, after transferring command of the

expedition from Sawkins to Coxon, the buccaneers set fire to Santa María and rowed downstream to the Pacific. They found a small bark in the river, and within a few days they had captured several piraguas, or large dugouts usually propelled by sail. Because of the varied speed of their transportation the pirates agreed to rendezvous near Panamá, some going first to the Pearl Islands while others followed the shore. The first pirate canoes containing some sixty-eight men led by Sawkins, Coxon, and Harris, came up to the city of Panamá early in the morning of May 3. They found five large ships and three barks off the port at Perico Island, commanded by Don Jacinto de Barahona, who had been placed in charge of the defenses of Panamá. The Spanish fighting force consisted of 228 men (mostly Negroes and mulattoes), all on the barks, leaving the larger ships unmanned.[32] After a bloody engagement lasting some five hours, one of the barks deserted and the others surrendered to the pirates. English casualties in the battle of Perico were twenty dead, including Captain Harris. The Spanish losses were greater, probably a hundred or more killed, among them the commander Barahona. After the battle the three large ships were also taken by the pirates without difficulty. The largest, "La Santísima Trinidad" of 400 tons, was converted into a buc-

---

[32] According to Ayres, *op. cit.,* 13, there were 200 pirates and 280 Spaniards in this engagement.

caneer flagship. She had nothing aboard but a cargo of provisions and a few cannon, but more guns were moved to her from the other ships.[33]

Now the English were in command of all the shipping in Panamá roads, more than they needed to carry them wherever they might want to cruise. They were dissuaded from attempting an assault on the city because of their small number and the strong fortifications, although such an attack might well have been successful. Most of the Spanish defense force was off in the interior fighting the Indians, and there were not enough soldiers left in the city to man the guns.

On May 5 Captain Coxon, who had quarreled with the other commanders, took one of the captured barks and seventy of his adherents to return to the Gulf of San Miguel and back to the Caribbean. Leadership of the expedition devolved again upon Richard Sawkins. On May 12 the pirates ran across to Taboga Island with the "Trinidad" and another ship of 180 tons, having set fire to the remaining prizes. While cruising off Taboga on May 20, Captain Sharp attacked and captured an unarmed king's vessel coming in from Peru, with 51,000 pieces of eight and some much appreciated supplies. Two other prizes were taken shortly

---

[33] Zaragoza, *Piraterías de los ingleses,* 157, quotes the president of the *audiencia* to the effect that the pirates found 50,000 pesos on the "Trinidad," but apparently he was referring to another ship taken on May 20 (see below). Ringrose (Esquemeling, *op. cit.,* 328, 336) says the "Trinidad" was taken later, at Pueblo Nuevo.

afterward, including a 100-ton bark to which Sharp transferred his crew.

After thoroughly rummaging the gardens of Taboga and exchanging some pompous correspondence with the president of Panamá, on May 23 or 25 the buccaneer squadron sailed for Coiba Island, still uninhabited and an excellent base for careening and mainland raids. En route one of the pirate barks was blown across the gulf and joined Coxon on his way back to the Caribbean, while another was recaptured by the Spaniards. While his somewhat diminished fleet lay at anchor off Coiba, on June 1, Sawkins crossed with sixty men to Pueblo Nuevo, on the south coast of Veragua. Here the Spaniards were forewarned and had thrown up a wooden breastwork on the bank of the river just below the village. In storming this improvised fort Sawkins and two others were killed, and the pirates were driven back. Before returning to Coiba they seized a 100-ton ship, loaded with corn, which was given the good English name "Mayflower."

Now Bartholomew Sharp was elected commander of the buccaneers. A dissident minority of sixty-three men refused to serve under him and were given a bark in which to return the way they had come. After two weeks at Coiba and the neighboring island of Quicara, or Jicarón, during which time they careened and took on water, wood, and a few provisions, the pirates sailed on June 16,

1680, for South America. They now numbered 146 men in two vessels, Sharp commanding the "Trinidad" and a Captain John Cox in the "Mayflower," Edmund Cook having been deposed in a mutiny.

For the next ten months Sharp and his men raided the west coast of South America. They sacked Ilo and La Serena (November-December, 1680), careened at Juan Fernández Island (January, 1681), and lost twenty-eight men during a raid at Arica (February). Sharp was turned out of his command, and reinstated when his successor was killed at Arica. Forty-four of his men rebelled, and on April 27 left their comrades at Plata Island off the coast of Ecuador, to make their way back to the Caribbean by way of the isthmus.

Captain Sharp was left with only sixty-five men in "La Santísima Trinidad." Until now his cruise had not been specially fortunate in acquiring loot, but soon after parting with the deserters Sharp took a valuable prize with a large amount of silver and gold, both in coin and ingots. On May 5, 1681, the buccaneers arrived off Caño Island, and on the sixteenth they entered the Gulf of Nicoya. There they lay three weeks, during which time they completely overhauled their ships, sacked and burned the town of Esparza, and captured a few small prizes.[34] Sharp left Nicoya on June 9, called again at Caño Island, and ran in to Dulce Gulf on the sixteenth. As there were no Spaniards nearby, the

---

[34] Bancroft, *Central America*, II, p. 541. Neither Ringrose nor Ayres mentions Esparza by name.

ships were careened and trimmed in that quiet bay.
On July 8 the buccaneers set sail and headed south
once again. They took another and even more
valuable prize off Peru, although later they were
much chagrined to learn that they had left behind
several hundred silver ingots which they thought
were tin! The "Trinidad" had an uneventful
voyage around Cape Horn and reached Barbados
on February 7, 1682.

From the Spanish point of view the cruise of
Sharp and his fellow buccaneers was disastrous.
The Spaniards estimated at more than 4,000,000
pesos the total damage done by this relatively small
pirate band to their shipping and port installations.
Twenty-five ships had been destroyed, a crippling
blow to commerce, and probably more than two
hundred Spaniards had been killed.[35] Faced with
this scourge, far worse than any previous attack on
the Pacific coast, the Spanish colonials showed
great bravery on occasion but were quite unable to
cope effectively with such an enemy. The royal
officials must have realized that the west coast was
without any real defense. The old procedure of
warning the Manila galleon and keeping the Pacific shores deserted was clearly not the way to
uphold Spain's proud dominion in her "private
sea." [36] But Spain was in a period of decline, mis-

[35] Artiñano, *Historia del Comercio*, 225.
[36] While Sharp was at Nicoya, in June, 1681, enemy ships were
reported seen on the coast just east of Acapulco. Nothing was done
other than strengthen the Acapulco garrison, since the Manila ship
was not due for another five months. Robles, *Diario*, I, p. 298. Letter
from viceroy, July 12, 1681, in *México* 52, AGI.

ruled by a feeble-minded king, and the colonial officials could only lament and hope that the buccaneer invasion was a transitory evil.

Sharp and some of his men later were tried for piracy, at the insistence of the Spanish ambassador in London, but they were acquitted for lack of evidence.[37] The buccaneers were becoming such a problem, particularly in the Caribbean, that in 1684 Spain's traditional enemies agreed at Ratisbon no longer to employ piracy as a means of dealing undercover blows. Many pirates were captured and hanged, or forced to take up a more honest profession. But before this news reached America the last and largest buccaneer invasion of the Pacific was under way.

Three English ships entered the Pacific in March, 1684, two of them through the Straits of Magellan and the third around Cape Horn. The "Nicholas" was a pirate ship out of London, with twenty-six guns and a crew of seventy, commanded by John Eaton. The "Cygnet," commanded by Captain Charles Swan, also hailed from London, having been fitted out by a company of English merchants for a contraband trading voyage to the Spanish colonies. She carried £5,000 in merchandise, sixteen guns, and a crew of about sixty, mostly Englishmen with a few Dutch and other nationalities. "Batchelor's Delight," perhaps one of the

---

[37] Masefield, *op. cit.,* 289.

most appropriately named of all buccaneer ships, had recently been taken as a prize off West Africa by a band of seventy pirates led by Edmund Cook. She had thirty-six guns and 180 tons burden. Cook had cruised before in the Pacific, in 1680-81, and with him were many of his old pirate followers including the journalists Dampier, Ringrose, and Wafer. William Ambrosia Cowley was master and pilot of the "Batchelor's Delight," and also wrote an account of his voyage.[38]

Swan, in the merchantman "Cygnet," cruised up the coast of Chile and Peru, but everywhere met with a hostile reception from the Spaniards. Some of his men were killed in a skirmish at Valdivia, Swan later using this as an excuse for turning pirate.[39] The viceroy of Peru ordered out a fleet to capture the intruders and sent warnings to Panamá and Mexico. By June, 1684, the whole west coast had been alerted to the presence of an enemy.[40]

Eaton and Cook, whose piratical designs were similar, kept company off South America and called at Juan Fernández (April), Lobos de

---

[38] A very detailed and highly readable account of a cruise with these pirates appears in Dampier, *New Voyage*. Dampier was with Cook and Davis until September, 1685, and then sailed with Swan. Another account was written by Wafer *(New Voyage)*, who stayed with Davis throughout his cruise. Cowley's journal (in Callander, *Terra Australis Cognita*, 529-538) describes the cruise of the "Batchelor's Delight" until September, 1684, when Cowley changed over to Eaton's ship.

[39] Dampier, *New Voyage*, 100, 137.

[40] *Ibid.*, 73. Zaragoza, *Piraterías de los ingleses*, 163. Robles, *Diario*, II, p. 69. The news reached Mexico City June 9.

Afuera (May), and the Galápagos Islands (June).
They took four prizes loaded with wood and provisions but no specie. Realizing that the Spaniards
would have taken steps to protect their silver shipments, the buccaneers next determined to raid the
coast of Central America. About the middle of
July, 1684, the two pirate ships with one of their
prizes arrived off the Gulf of Nicoya, where Captain Cook died. When he was taken ashore to be
buried just inside the gulf, the pirates seized two
mestizos who led them to a cattle *estancia*. A party
of twelve men left to round up some beef was
surprised by forty or fifty Spaniards and almost
captured.[41]

The pirate crews spent about two weeks in the
Gulf of Nicoya, taking on wood and water and
rummaging the countryside. On July 29, in accordance with buccaneer procedure, the men of
the "Batchelor's Delight" elected as their captain
Edward Davis, who had been quartermaster.[42] The
next day the three ships sailed out of Nicoya for
Realejo, where they arrived on August 2. Intend-
ing to seize the town, the buccaneers anchored and
took their boats into the harbor. They soon discovered that the Spaniards were prepared for
them, having erected breastworks along the two
river approaches to Realejo, and consequently the
pirates withdrew to their ships.[43]

[41] Dampier, *op. cit.*, 83-87.
[42] According to Lussan, *Journal*, 68, and Fernández Duro, *Armada Española*, v, p. 299, Davis was Flemish.
[43] Dampier, *op. cit.*, 85-90.

On August 5, Davis and Eaton sailed from
Realejo toward Amapala Bay, or the Gulf of
Fonseca. The next day Davis took some men in
the ships' boats and landed first on Meanguera
Island and then on Amapala, capturing a priest
and antagonizing the Indians. The ships followed
in and were careened, trimmed, and victualed
while lying some five weeks at Amapala Island,
unmolested by the Spaniards. Eaton and Davis,
not agreeing on the course next to be followed,
determined to separate. The former hoisted sail on
the "Nicholas" and sailed from Amapala southward, on September 12.[44] He called briefly at
Cocos Isand, continued cruising off Peru, and
started west across the Pacific about the end of
November, 1684.[45] Davis, in the "Batchelor's Delight," left Amapala on September 13 and set
course for Peru.[46]

Meanwhile the contraband trader Swan in his
ship "Cygnet," having been unable to dispose of
his cargo in South America, came up to Nicoya
probably about the same time that Davis and
Eaton were careening nearby at Amapala. There
he found still another pirate gang which had recently crossed overland from the Caribbean and
had seized the mining camp of Santa María,
getting away with 120 pounds of gold. These men
were led by Peter Harris, nephew of the bucca-

[44] *Ibid.*, 92-95. Callander, *op. cit.*, II, p. 537. According to Cowley,
Eaton sailed in mid-August (late August, N. S.)
[45] Callander, *op. cit.*, II, pp. 537-538. Dampier, *op. cit.*, 96.
[46] Dampier, *op. cit.*, 95.

neer of the same name who was killed at Panamá in 1680. Harris had been following the coast in piraguas hoping to seize a ship.[47]

Charles Swan is described by Dampier as a fat, temperamental martinet who had no stomach for piracy and on the whole seems to have been pretty much of a coward, although brutal enough when he had the upper hand.[48] There was little discipline among his rowdy crewmen, and whenever enough of them banded together he always bowed to their will. Now with the influence of Harris's buccaneers, the "Cygnet's" men insisted on becoming pirates as well. Consequently Swan gave Harris a small bark he had captured, and the two ships turned south to join Davis at Plata Island in mid-October. The three buccaneers then made some profitless raids in Ecuador before turning northward again toward Panamá in January, 1685.[49]

In the meantime the west coast of Central America was being plagued with still another small group of buccaneers. William Knight and his men crossed the Isthmus of Panamá, probably in September-October, 1684, and cruised about in piraguas until they succeeded in capturing a Spanish ship off Acajutla. Knight continued harassing the ports and shipping of Central America, taking other prizes, until perhaps February or March,

47 *Ibid.,* 100, 114, 138.
48 *Ibid., passim.*
49 *Ibid.,* 116.

1685, when he sailed for Guayaquil. His crew
was composed of forty-five English and twelve
French buccaneers. Later Knight was to return
north and join forces with Davis and the others.[50]

Swan, Davis, and Harris spent the early months
of 1685 together in the Gulf of Panamá, cleaning
their ships' bottoms in the Pearl Islands and waiting for the silver fleet to come up from Peru. The
fleet had not sailed for several years, but now the
viceroy fitted out a squadron of seven ships commanded jointly by his brother-in-law Don Tomás
Palavicino, Don Pedro Pontejos, and Don Antonio de Beas. The Spaniards had two large ships
mounting forty guns each, two others of twenty-
six and fourteen guns respectively, and three converted merchant ships without ordnance, with a
total force of over two thousand men.[51]

While these warlike preparations were going
on, the buccaneers were joined by welcome reinforcements from the Caribbean. Pirates in that sea
were having a difficult time since the Peace of
Ratisbon, as they could no longer rely on the con-
nivance of their own governments in their rob-
beries. François Grogniet, with two hundred
French and eighty English pirates, crossed the
isthmus in February-March, 1685, secured pira-

---

[50] *Ibid.,* 147, 151.
[51] Fernández Duro, *Armada Española,* v, pp. 300-301. Zaragoza,
Piraterías de los ingleses, 163. However, Dampier, *op. cit.,* 147, says
the Spaniards had fourteen sail plus piraguas, with a total of 174
guns and 3,000 men. Lussan, *Journal,* 86-87, gives the Spanish armament as 156 guns. Burney, *Chronological History,* IV, p. 177, estimates
the number of men at 2,500, more than half of them Indians or slaves.

guas to transport his men, and joined Davis and Swan at Taboga Island about March 10. Grogniet was given a prize bark, and the pirate fleet sailed across the gulf to meet another newly-arrived group of 180 English pirates led by a Captain Townley.[52] Townley had visited the now deserted mines of Santa María, and had already taken two small barks on their way up from Peru. On April 21 a third party of 264 buccaneers, mostly Frenchmen, under Captains Rose, Desmarais, and le Picard, also joined the pirate fleet, having crossed the isthmus a few days before.[53]

From prisoners taken from the Spanish prizes the pirates learned that the plate fleet was on its way north. The buccaneer squadron now consisted of five large ships and five barks, in addition to a number of piraguas or large sailing canoes, with a total force of 960 well-armed men, about two-thirds English and a third Frenchmen. However only two of the ships, the "Cygnet" and the "Batchelor's Delight," had great ordnance, fifty-two guns altogether.[54]

On June 7, 1685, the Spanish fleet appeared around the north end of the Pearl Islands, having first secretly landed the cargo of silver (estimated by Dampier at 12,000,000 pieces of eight) on the mainland. The pirates were to windward, and chased the Spaniards until dark, but during the

---

[52] Dampier, *op. cit.,* 136-139.

[53] Lussan, *Journal,* 55-67.

[54] *Ibid.,* 67-68, 80. Dampier, *op. cit.,* 147.

night the latter employed a decoy light and moved around into the wind so that the following morning they had the weather gauge over the pirates. With a far weaker armament, the buccaneers could do nothing but try to escape. The Spanish warships pursued them most of the day and inflicted some damage with their cannon, but finally the pirates got away. There were few casualties on either side. The English blamed their defeat on their loss of the weather gauge and on the fact that Grogniet's ship did not enter the fight.[55] According to the Spanish account only lack of coordination among their three generals kept them from completely destroying the enemy.[56]

After the battle of Panamá the buccaneers retired from the gulf and rendezvoused at deserted Coiba Island toward the end of June. There they remained somewhat over a month, repairing their battered ships, making additional piraguas, taking on water and stores, and debating their future moves. A party of 150 men was sent on an unproductive raid to Pueblo Nuevo, on the mainland, early in July. On the fifteenth of that month the buccaneers were joined by William Knight and his crew, who had just come up from the coast of Peru. At this point there was a falling out between the English and French pirates, the former sulkily moving off to a different part of the island. Dampier says the quarrel was due to Grogniet's

---

[55] Dampier, *op. cit.*, 146-148. Lussan, *op. cit.*, 81-87.
[56] Fernández Duro, *op. cit.*, v, p. 301. Zaragoza, *op. cit.*, 163.

cowardly behavior in the recent battle, while the French pirate de Lussan blames it all on the haughty attitude of the English and their sacrilegious pillaging of churches, which greatly shocked and offended the Catholic French buccaneers.[57]

The Frenchmen under Grogniet, numbering 340 men, remained on Coiba until October, 1685, using that island as a base for raids on the Veragua coast. Meanwhile, on July 30, Davis, Swan, Townley and Knight, with 640 men in eight ships, sailed northward. The English realized that there would be little profit in further raids on shipping, and determined to attack the coastal settlements of Nicaragua. Arriving off Realejo, they left a crew to man the anchored ships while 470 buccaneers went ashore and marched twenty miles to the city of León, capital of the province. León was defended by a superior force of Spaniards, but the pirates drove them off in a brief engagement on August 21. There was little booty to be taken, and the governor was slow in providing the demanded ransom, so after three days' occupation León was put to the torch and the buccaneers retired to the coast. On August 27 the same landing party seized the town of Realejo almost without opposition, finding the place deserted and empty of loot except for a quantity of supplies and rigging. They rum-

[57] Dampier, *op. cit.*, 149-152. Lussan, *op. cit.*, 87-89. The Protestant English buccaneers observed religious ceremonies on their ships in most cases.

maged the surrounding farms and cattle ranches, set fire to the town, and retired aboard their ships on September 3.[58]

At Realejo there was a further division among the buccaneer captains. Davis, Knight, and Harris, with four ships and three hundred men, sailed on September 7 with the intention of returning to Peru, but an epidemic of "spotted fever" broke out, evidently contracted during the raid in Nicaragua, and they decided to put in at Amapala Bay. There they lay several weeks at a small island where the sick, almost half the crews, were set ashore. Many of them died. Unmolested by the Spaniards, the pirates made a few raids on the mainland and rounded up some cattle. Toward the end of September the fleet sailed from Amapala and ran south to Cocos Island, where they took on water and a quantity of coconuts. Harris, with two ships, sailed west from Cocos to cross the Pacific, while Knight and Davis stayed together off the coast of South America for another year. They careened in the Galápagos Islands, had several engagements with the Spaniards in Peru, took a few prizes, and parted company at Juan Fernández Island in November, 1686. Knight then returned to the Atlantic, while Davis with eighty men, in the old "Batchelor's Delight," continued on the coast of Peru for still another year. After a final careening at Juan Fernández he rounded Cape

---

[58] Dampier, *op. cit.,* 152-57.

Horn, at the end of 1687, and returned to the Caribbean.[59]

Meanwhile Swan and Townley, with 340 men in their two ships and two small prizes, decided to cruise northward for the Manila galleon. While still at Realejo they were afflicted by the same epidemic fever which struck Davis and the others. However they could not linger in a hostile and populous country, and on September 13, 1685, they hoisted sail and headed westerly up the coast. In early October Townley went ashore with 106 men near Tehuantepec to look for provisions, but they were set upon by two hundred Spaniards and Indians. Dampier (who was not in the landing party) says that the Spaniards were quickly repulsed "and made greater speed back than they had done forward." [60] The Spanish account states laconically that the pirates "were forced to go elsewhere." [61] No one seems to have been hurt.

On October 13 the pirate fleet dropped anchor in the now deserted port of Guatulco. Here they remained over a week while the sick were taken ashore, and Townley led rummaging parties into the interior. On one of them they visited an Indian village, probably Santa María Guatulco, but they saw no Spaniards. During their stay the pirates mended their sails, filled the water casks, cut wood

---

[59] Wafer, *New Voyage,* 112-128.
[60] Dampier, *op. cit.,* 163.
[61] Robles, *Diario,* II, p. 104.

for the ships' fires, and caught turtles. They sailed from Guatulco on October 22.[62]

Recovered from their fever, the buccaneers beat up along the coast behind their piraguas, which were sent ahead to try to take prisoners. From November 1 to 6 the pirate fleet called at Puerto Angel, where they found a deserted cattle *estancia* two leagues away. The men gorged themselves on beef, pork, and chickens, and took a few provisions back to the ships. Two of the canoes reached Acapulco about the end of October and were seen there by the Spaniards.[63] On their return to join the ships the piraguas had made two landings through the heavy surf. The first was at the mouth of a river, probably the Ometepec, where they filled their water casks before an audience of Spaniards, who fired at them. The second landing was at a lagoon in which the pirates were trapped for two days, when the Spaniards stationed themselves at the outlet.[64]

On November 13 the buccaneers went ashore in force in the estuary of the Ometepec River, and drove off a large body of Spaniards who were waiting behind an improvised breastwork. A foraging party here took a mulatto prisoner who told them about a ship recently arrived at Acapulco, and Townley conceived the ambition to take her as

[62] Dampier, *op. cit.*, 163-166.
[63] Robles, *op. cit.*, II, p. 105.
[64] Dampier, *op. cit.*, 166-169.

a prize, being dissatisfied with his own vessel.[65] In the evening of November 17, within sight of the Paps of Acapulco, Townley put off with 140 men in twelve canoes, and the following day he landed at Puerto Marqués. During the night of November 19-20 the pirates rowed across to the inner harbor of Acapulco and found the desired prize anchored directly beneath the castle of San Diego. It was clearly impossible to cut the ship out without being blasted by the fort, so Townley contented himself with getting a good view of the town and castle in the early dawn before returning aboard his vessel.[66] The pirates closely followed the shore west of Acapulco, making a raid on the village of Petatlán, passing Zihuatanejo (November 23), and calling at Ixtapa, where they secured some beef and took a mule train with a quantity of provisions. Swan kept as a servant a mulatto boy he captured at Ixtapa.[67]

Meanwhile in Mexico City the viceroy had been informed of the pirates' activities and took steps to defend the Manila galleon. He ordered Admiral Isidro Atondo y Antillón, who had just returned from a pearling expedition to Lower California, to go out in his little *balandra* and escort the ship expected from China. Atondo sailed from Matanchel on November 25 and crossed in only three

[65] *Ibid.*, 169-170.
[66] *Ibid.*, 170-172.
[67] *Ibid.*, 172-175. Robles, *Diario*, II, p. 106, says that news of an enemy off Colima reached Mexico City on November 19. Perhaps the pirates had sent canoes ahead.

CAPTAIN SWAN'S "CYGNET" AT IXTAPA
From a contemporary engraving.

AMBUSH OF SWAN'S RAIDERS NEAR SENTICPAC
From a contemporary engraving.

days to Cape San Lucas, where the Manila galleon "Santa Rosa" had just arrived, an amazing coincidence. The two vessels crossed the mouth of the gulf, reaching Salagua on December 8, Zihuatanejo on the 18th, and Acapulco on the 20th.[68] How they managed to avoid Swan and Townley, whom they must have passed just south of Salagua, is a mystery. Possibly they slipped by each other during the night of December 9-10. In Mexico the galleon's escape was considered a miracle.

The pirate fleet went in to Salagua on December 11, and the next morning two hundred men landed and routed a "large" war party on the beach. Here they took prisoners who disclosed some helpful information about the countryside, but made no mention of the fact that the Manila ship had been in this same bay just three days before. Clearly the buccaneers lacked a good interrogator. Still sanguine with the thought of capturing this rich prize, they sailed from Salagua on December 16 and strung out their ships for a distance of ten leagues off Cape Corrientes. Four of Townley's canoes were sent in to Valle de Banderas to look for provisions. This landing party skirmished with some Spaniards, losing four men and killing eighteen of the enemy. On December 28 the pirates had to abandon their blockade and run down to Chamela Bay for water and wood, leaving Townley ashore with sixty men to rummage the countryside. The

---

[68] Letter from viceroy, March 28, 1686, in *México* 55, AGI.

fleet returned northward and entered Valle de Banderas on January 11, 1686.[69]

After spending six days at Banderas, killing and salting beef in sight of "great Companies" of Spaniards, the buccaneers split into two groups. Swan and his men, assuming now that the Manila ship had escaped them while they were busy taking on provisions, rather unreasonably laid all the blame on Townley for having wasted time in Acapulco when they could have been victualing. Swan wanted to raid the coast northward, while Townley was for returning south. The two captains parted ways on January 17 and sailed from Banderas Bay, each with one ship and a small bark, Swan with two hundred men and Townley with 120.[70]

From the pirates' point of view, Swan's cruise north from Cape Corrientes was a serious mistake. On January 30, 1686, his ships anchored behind the islands of Mazatlán (misnamed "Islands Chametly" but clearly identified by Dampier). Here Swan took a hundred men in canoes for about thirty leagues northward along the coast. They landed at several points, but found that there were no rich mines or towns as they had expected. To the contrary, the cattle had been driven inland and the whole countryside was at arms. On February 12, eighty pirates landed at the mouth of

[69] Dampier, *op. cit.,* 177-181.
[70] *Ibid.,* 181-182.

the Chametla (Baluarte) River and marched to Rosario, where they stole eighty or ninety bushels of maize. Seventy men were sent into Río Grande de Santiago on the twenty-first, and from a prisoner they heard of the town of Senticpac fifteen miles inland. Swan, still badly in need of supplies for his voyage across the Pacific, went with 140 men in eight canoes up the river and marched overland, taking Senticpac without resistance on February 26. They found a good supply of maize and began to transfer it on horses to the canoes. While they were doing this a large party of Spaniards carried out an ambush and succeeded in killing fifty of the buccaneers, one-fourth of Swan's entire force. The forlorn survivors returned to their canoes and paddled down to the waiting ships.[71]

On March 3 Swan left the mainland and set course for Lower California. However, he was driven back to the Tres Marías Islands, where he spent almost three weeks (March 17-April 5) at the east end of María Magdalena careening his two vessels. They returned to Valle de Banderas to take on water, and on April 10, 1686, the pirate ships cleared Cape Corrientes and began the long voyage across the Pacific.[72]

---

[71] *Ibid.*, 182-189. Basil Ringrose, the chronicler of Sharp's expedition, was one of those killed. *Cf.* Robles, *Diario,* II, p. 116. The latter says Swan had released twenty prisoners before this battle, and the pirates "are perishing of hunger, and eat dogs, cats, and horses."

[72] Dampier, *op. cit.,* 190-194. Swan's crew mutinied in the Philippines, and soon afterward Swan was killed. Dampier and others of the crew reached England in another ship.

After parting company with Swan, Townley was seen off Zacatula early in February, 1686.[73] A few days later, twenty leagues from Acapulco, he set his prisoners ashore and burned his smaller ship. Perhaps she was in bad condition, or he no longer needed her with such a reduced crew. Four of Townley's men were captured by the Spaniards somewhere along this coast and were taken to Mexico City the following April.[74] The next notice we have of Townley is when he arrived off Nicoya in March, 1686.

François Grogniet, whom we left with 340 French buccaneers on Coiba Island in July, 1685, was probably one of the most unsuccessful pirate captains in history. When the English deserted him he had three small ships and a few piraguas. The problem which bothered him to the exclusion of all others was that of finding enough provisions to keep his men from starving. The few Spanish settlements along the coast of Veragua had been alerted, cattle had been moved inland, and look-outs were stationed along the shore. Whenever the pirates were sighted everyone fled, carrying their food and valuables with them and destroying what had to be left behind. Grogniet would not allow his men to waste precious gunpowder in hunting, and they do not seem to have been very adept

---

[73] Letter from viceroy, February 16, 1686, in *México* 55, AGI.
[74] Robles, *Diario*, II, pp. 115, 119.

fishermen. Consequently they were always on the verge of starvation.[75]

In August-September, 1685, Grogniet and 120 of his men made a raid along the coast to the east, pillaging the ranches and taking two barks loaded with corn, more appreciated than gold by the famished buccaneers. During the absence of this group their comrades attacked Pueblo Nuevo for the second time in two months, but found nothing of value. Early in September a sugar cane mill near Santiago Veragua was looted. After cleaning and repairing their ships the pirates got away from Coiba Island on October 8, arriving off Realejo two weeks later. Bad weather kept the canoes from getting into the harbor until November 1. They found the breastworks across the creek unmanned and partially destroyed, and the town of Realejo abandoned, the result of the recent English raid. On approaching León the buccaneers were told that a force of two thousand defended the city, so they changed their plans, reembarked on November 10, and sailed out of Realejo. The next few days were spent in raiding deserted farms near the coast. On November 14 a force of 150 pirates

---

[75] For the activities of the French buccaneers, almost our only source is Lussan, *Journal.* It is somewhat confusing as far as geographical names are concerned, and it is not always clear where the raids mentioned took place, nor whether they were made by the main body of pirates or a small detached group. On the other hand, the *Journal* makes good reading and contains many details of pirate life not given here.

captured Pueblo Viejo (a small town north of Realejo) after some fighting, and found a quantity of provisions. On another raid they took prisoners, and later killed some of them when the required ransom of provisions did not arrive. On November 24 the Frenchmen received a letter from the Spaniards, informing them that a brief war between their countries had ended, and suggesting that they return to the Caribbean under safe-conduct. No doubt Grogniet would have liked to do this, but some of his men feared a trap (they did not even know that there had been a war), and the offer was not accepted.[76]

The buccaneers sailed from the coast of Nicaragua on November 28, after setting ashore thirty prisoners. The raid had been a dismal failure. The Spaniards were everywhere at arms and had left practically nothing for the pirates to steal. On December 5 Grogniet sent seventy-one men in three canoes into Culebra Bay, above Nicoya, to rummage unsuccessfully for provisions. Four days later they went around to the Gulf of Nicoya and dropped anchor in Caldera Bay, but the party sent to sack Esparza returned empty-handed when informed that the town was strongly defended. The pirates caught a few horses and ate them, and later they found some plantains growing along the shore.[77]

[76] Lussan, *op. cit.*, 93-104. War had broken out the previous year between Spain and France.
[77] *Ibid.*, 105-107.

From Nicoya the hungry Frenchmen cruised southward to "Chiriquita," probably Santiago Alanje or Chiriquí, in Veragua province. The landing party was driven off by a large force of Spaniards on December 22. Back at Coiba Island, the pirates organized a second attempt on Chiriquita which was carried out with success by 230 men before dawn on January 9, 1686. They killed a number of Spaniards, took others as hostages, and burned all the houses. After a week the demanded ransom of food was provided and the buccaneers returned to Coiba. Toward the end of the month a Spanish punitive expedition landed at the pirates' camp and burned their only large ship while the Frenchmen hid nearby in two small barks. The latter were now of little use as they had no sails.[78]

Grogniet now desperately decided on still another raid to Nicaragua. On March 14, 1686, he departed from Coiba with his three hundred surviving pirates in the two barks, a forty-oar galiot, and assorted piraguas and other small craft. A party was dispatched to rummage Pueblo Nuevo again, but they lost four dead and thirty-three wounded in an engagement with a Spanish warship stationed at the mouth of the river. Other raids, largely unproductive, were then made along the shore to the west. Esparza was found to be empty of stores and inhabitants, the latter having retired to Cartago. On March 23 Grogniet's forces,

---

[78] *Ibid.*, 108-117.

then in the Gulf of Nicoya, were met by those of
Captain Townley, who had just returned from his
cruise up the coast with Swan. The two pirate
gangs joined forces and set out in their canoes on
the projected raid to Nicaragua, leaving a few
men to guard the ships.[79]

The buccaneer force, consisting of 345 men,
landed at a deserted point and marched to Granada,
which was taken against a spirited resistance on
April 10, 1686. A number of forts or breastworks
had been erected and the Spaniards had a dozen
or more cannon. Pirate losses in this fight were
four dead, the enemy as usual "having lost many
men." After the battle the pious buccaneers, or at
least the Frenchmen, went en masse to the cathedral
and chanted a victorious *Te Deum*. But after all
it was a hollow victory. Again the Spaniards had
removed all but a few supplies, while the more
valuable treasures had been taken out to an island
in Lake Nicaragua. Since no ransom was forth-
coming, the torch was applied to the houses. The
pirates left Granada on April 15, still as hungry
and as poor as ever, and marched back to the coast
through Masaya, harassed by "twenty-five hundred
Spanish." [80] By April 26 the last pirate stragglers
reached the shore and embarked for Realejo, where
they cast anchor two days later. Pueblo Viejo was
captured a second time on April 28, and Chinan-

[79] *Ibid.,* 118-123.
[80] *Ibid.,* 123-129, 182-183.

dega was sacked and burned on May 5. As usual the Spaniards had carried away or destroyed all provisions.[81]

Back on their ships in the harbor of Realejo the buccaneers distributed 7,600 pesos to ten permanently disabled members of their party, in accordance with the standard pirate agreement. De Lussan mentions that this was "practically all the money we had saved," a slim enough reward for more than a year's buccaneering.[82] At this low point in their fortunes Townley and Grogniet decided to part company. Half of the Frenchmen, 148 buccaneers, elected to go to Panamá with Townley and his crew of 115. About 145 French pirates stayed with Grogniet, who wished to spend the rainy season at Amapala Bay and cross back to the Caribbean as soon as possible. On May 19, 1686, the pirate flotillas sailed and paddled from Realejo on their respective courses.[83]

Little is known about Grogniet's activities during the next eight months. Apparently he spent most of this time on one of the islands in the Bay of Amapala. Soon after arriving there, 112 pirates marched inland and secured 450 pounds of gold at a mining camp halfway to Tegucigalpa. Later

---

[81] *Ibid.,* 133-135.

[82] In addition to the common fund, individual pirates kept jewels and other valuable objects which served as stakes in the principal diversion, gambling. De Lussan mentions that silver was not greatly appreciated and was often left behind because of its weight.

[83] Lussan, *op. cit.,* 135-137. De Lussan went off with Townley at this point.

they took their canoes up the river to Pueblo Viejo, in Nicaragua, which was sacked for the third time. More than half of Grogniet's men deserted and sailed for the north in a bark and several piraguas, probably in June or July of 1686. Part of this group stayed in the Tres Marías Islands for more than three years. Since they were the last of the buccaneers to remain in the Pacific, their activities will be narrated at the end of this chapter.[84]

Townley, with two ships and 260 men, spent three days at Culebra Bay where at last a good quantity of food was discovered in three farms nearby. He then ran southward to Coiba Island where he took on water and wood. On June 13 the pirates sailed from Coiba, and ten days later they landed in force and seized and burned a place called "Villia" (la Villa de los Santos) on the west side of the Gulf of Panamá. Here they found 15,000 pesos in gold and silver, but lost it all as well as some of their men when they were ambushed by the Spaniards. Altogether fourteen pirates were killed in this encounter. In retaliation the buccaneers decapitated four of their prisoners on the spot, and two more when the *alcalde mayor* quibbled over ransom terms. This seems to have impressed the Spaniards, who gave up 11,000 pesos and a hundred pounds of nails, together with some supplies, in return for the remaining prisoners.[85]

[84] *Ibid.*, 188-191.
[85] *Ibid.*, 137-147.

On July 4, 1686, Townley and his fleet left the vicinity of Villa de los Santos and cruised about looking for a safe place to take on water. On the twenty-second they captured a small bark off the Pearl, or King's, Islands. Early in August they took another prize in Panamá harbor and rummaged Taboga Island; at the same time the pirate galiot went into the Chepó River and captured a Spanish bark. For the next several months Panamá was virtually blockaded, and commerce was at a standstill. From Taboga the buccaneers sent a message to the president of the *audiencia* demanding the return of a Frenchman and four English pirates who had been captured, in exchange for fifty Spanish prisoners. Receiving no answer, they repaired their ships in the Pearl Islands while a party was sent into the Gulf of San Miguel on August 9-14. The latter group captured a bark and had a brush with the Spaniards who, de Lussan reports, left "many dead and wounded." [86]

Within the last few months it would seem that the Spanish authorities in Panamá had made peace with the Indians in the wild country beyond Chepó. Consequently the route recently used by the pirates to get between the Caribbean and the Pacific was effectively closed to them, several invading parties having been captured and killed by the Spaniards and their new allies.

Meanwhile two ships and a longboat were being

[86] *Ibid.*, 153-156.

armed and prepared at Panamá to go out against
the buccaneers. At dawn on August 22, 1686, the
opponents met off Taboga Island, and a battle
ensued which lasted until after noon. The pirates
seem to have carried the day, as they captured both
Spanish ships and ran the longboat ashore. De
Lussan tells us that about a hundred Spaniards
were killed or wounded. The pirates had one
killed and twenty-two wounded, most of the latter
dying shortly thereafter. The reason for this high
mortality, again according to de Lussan, was that
the Spaniards had poisoned their bullets! Captain
Townley was among the injured, and died on
September 9.[87]

Recuperating from the fray, the buccaneers at
Taboga Island sent another letter to the president
of Panamá demanding immediate return of the
five captive pirates. This was coldly refused by
the president, while a letter from the bishop of
Panamá, somewhat more conciliatory, explained
that the captives did not wish to be released as they
were Roman Catholics. Infuriated by these dilatory
tactics, Townley's men decapitated twenty of their
Spanish prisoners and sent their heads to the president, with the warning that ninety others would
receive the same treatment if he did not release
their men within twenty-four hours. The horrified
president sent out the five prisoners, whereupon
the pirates released twelve Spaniards and de-

[87] *Ibid.,* 158-163, 183-184.

manded 20,000 pesos to ransom the others. On September 4 the exchange took place, although the ransom had dwindled to 10,000 pieces of eight.[88]

Upon Townley's death the French captain le Picard was elected to command the pirate squadron. After a call at Otoque Island, the fleet moved out to the Pearl archipelago on September 10 and lay there over a month careening and victualing. During this time the pirates captured another prize with provisions from Natá. With a final raid on a sugar mill near Panamá City and on the town of Los Santos in late October, the fleet retired from the gulf and arrived off Coiba Island once again on November 16, 1686.[89]

At this time the pirate squadron consisted of several barks, a galiot, and a good number of piraguas and smaller dugout canoes. They were weak in artillery, having only four cannon and a few bow chasers. The total force had decreased to some 240 men, about fifty English and the rest French. De Lussan states that the Spaniards at Panamá had two three-decked ships with eighteen guns each, and a fifty-two-oar galley armed with five cannon and four swivel guns.[90]

On November 20 the pirate band left Coiba for the Veragua mainland, where more prisoners were taken and a few small settlements were rummaged. That there was still friction between the French

---

[88] *Ibid.*, 163-166.
[89] *Ibid.*, 166-174.
[90] *Ibid.*, 171, 174.

and English is suggested by the fact that the latter insisted on a division of boats and artillery between the two nationalities, which was carried out. On December 11, 1686, the buccaneer fleet entered "Boca del Toro bay," which from de Lussan's description can be identified as Dulce Gulf, in southern Costa Rica. They found the surrounding country deserted except for Indians hostile to the Spaniards, although the trail between Panamá and Guatemala was only six leagues inland. Here the pirates lay for three weeks careening their vessels and making additional dugouts.[91]

The next place called at was the Gulf of Nicoya. The fleet arrived off a mangrove swamp at the head of the gulf on January 6, 1687, and on landing the pirates found themselves up to their necks in mud. Regaining their ships, they entered the river and marched overland five leagues to the town of Nicoya, on January 7. The place was taken after some resistance and sacked of provisions and silver, after which the pirates returned aboard their ships with prisoners to await the usual ransom. From January 22 until mid-February the ships were careened on a small island in the gulf, while raiding parties visited Esparza and scoured the countryside for provisions. Nicoya was burned on February 16, its inhabitants having failed to provide the ransom demanded. On January 26, le Picard's group was joined by François Grogniet

---

[91] *Ibid.,* 174-179.

and his fifty-odd buccaneers, who had just coasted down from Amapala in three canoes.[92]

Having thoroughly exhausted the possibilities of Central America as far as loot and even subsistence were concerned, the buccaneers decided on a raid toward Guayaquil, far to the south. In the discussion of this project there was a falling out between two factions, and as a result Grogniet was joined by all the English and fifty of le Picard's Frenchmen. On February 24, 1687, both parties, each with a small ship, sailed from Nicoya. Grogniet had a total force of 142, and le Picard 160 buccaneers. The English pirates were led by a Georges d'Hout, alias George Huff.[93]

For four months the much-punished west coast of Central America was free from the scourge of pirates. In Ecuador, Guayaquil was looted in a successful and profitable raid, Grogniet was killed, and most of the English moved over to Edward Davis, who had come up in the "Batchelor's Delight." Le Picard was now in command of about 260 men, including twenty French pirates who had been with Davis.[94]

Le Picard's five small ships (he had taken several prizes) were badly damaged in a battle with the Spaniards off Ecuador at the end of May. Unwilling to risk the long trip around South America, the pirates determined to return to Cen-

[92] *Ibid.*, 179-195.
[93] *Ibid.*, 196. Burney, *Chronological History*, iv, p. 285.
[94] Lussan, *op. cit.*, 196-228.

tral America in order to cross overland to the
Caribbean at the first opportunity. On July 16,
1687, the mountains behind Realejo again came
into view, and the buccaneer squadron set course
for the Bay of Amapala, anchoring off Tigre
Island on July 23. All the islands in the bay were
now deserted, following the Spanish policy of
leaving nothing for the pirates to steal. Two weeks
later le Picard was joined by thirty of the buccaneers who had gone off with Grogniet's bark a
year before. They had turned back in the vicinity
of Acapulco and reached Amapala some months
previously. After a battle with the Spaniards they
had been hiding out in the islands of the bay, while
a large war galley and several Spanish piraguas
prowled about looking for them.[95]

Now le Picard, having careened his vessels,
decided to cruise northwest in search of the French
pirates who were still on the coast of Mexico. On
August 10, 1687, the buccaneer fleet sailed from
Amapala, passed Acajutla, and arrived off Tehuantepec on the twenty-seventh. A raiding party of
180 men was detached in canoes, landing through
the surf and marching to the town of Tehuantepec,
which they captured after several hours' brisk
fighting on August 30. The pirates abandoned the
city on September 3 without collecting the ransom
they had demanded.[96]

---

[95] *Ibid.*, 228-236.
[96] *Ibid.*, 236-239. *México* 57, AGI. Robles, *Diario*, II, p. 147.

Meanwhile the ships had gone into the deserted harbor of Guatulco, and their crews were laying waste the countryside looking for provisions. The buccaneers seem to have used Guatulco as a base of operations for almost three months. Their raids extended west to within twenty leagues of Acapulco, and east to Huamelula. On November 20, having failed to find their comrades or to acquire much loot, they weighed anchor and sailed back toward Amapala. On the return voyage one of the piraguas went in shore to an estuary "fifteen leagues to the leeward of Sonsonate" (Iztapa?), where there was a shipyard. They had a scrape with the Spaniards there, on December 10, and made off with some supplies and rigging. About the middle of December, 1687, the fleet dropped anchor once more in Amapala Bay.[97]

The buccaneers were now determined to march back across Central America to the North Sea. Long hours were spent making preparations for the difficult passage and torturing prisoners to get information regarding the best route. On December 24 the ships were scuttled, and on January 2, 1688, the 280 buccaneers began their march inland to the headwaters of the Segovia River. After a two-month trek most of them arrived at Cape Gracias a Dios, on the shore of the Caribbean.[98]

[97] Lussan, *op. cit.*, 239-247.
[98] *Ibid.*, 247-284.

The only pirates now remaining in the Spanish Pacific were a tiny band which, it will be remembered, had deserted from Grogniet in June or July of 1686 to try their luck in the direction of California. We have seen that thirty of these pirates became disheartened and turned back to Amapala. The remaining fifty-five, in their "rotten little bark which could not carry them far without splitting in two," beat up to windward until they arrived at the Tres Marías Islands, probably in the fall of 1686.[99]

News of the arrival of another enemy caused the expected reaction in New Spain. Garrisons in the few coastal towns were strengthened, and ranchers were ordered to move their cattle inland. The viceroy sent out a small vessel to warn the eastbound Manila galleon. This ship went to San Lucas and returned to Acapulco on February 25, 1687, without meeting either pirates or galleon, the sailing of the latter having been canceled.[100]

The buccaneers found in the Tres Marías group a fine refuge and base for mainland raids. The islands were uninhabited and rarely visited by the Spaniards, who in any event had few ships to send out. There were fresh water and plenty of fish and

---

[99] Lussan (1689 ed.), 348-349. Burney, *op. cit.*, IV, p. 295. Robles, *Diario*, II, p. 123. Robles says three enemy ships appeared off Guatulco in July, 1686, complementing de Lussan's statement that the pirates made a single landing in southern Mexico. Three strange ships were reported off the coast of Nueva Galicia in December, 1686 (*México* 57, AGI.)

[100] *México* 57, AGI.

small game, and a grove of "strait large Cedars"
which could be used for building additional
piraguas.[101] There were harbors and beaches for
careening. Cape Corrientes, on the track of the
Manila galleon, was only seventy miles away, a
good day's sail. It would seem that the Tres Marías
buccaneers spent several months repairing their
little ship and enlarging their fleet of piraguas.
There is some indication that they received reinforcements of men and an additional vessel.[102]
The earliest account we have of their activities is
for the year after their arrival, 1687. There are
records of two raids, one at Mazatlán (exact date
not known) and another at Navidad in September
of that year. At the port of Mazatlán "more than
a hundred" pirates (according to the Spanish
version) landed and marched inland to the presidio. The small garrison retreated while the
pirates took possession of the settlement for three
days. Before returning to the coast they burned
the church and houses in retaliation for the Spaniards' failure to provide ransom.[103] The second
raid occurred at Navidad Bay about the middle
of September. Eight piraguas of pirates entered

101 Dampier, *New Voyage*, 191.

102 It would seem that about forty French pirates came around
South America in a 100-ton ship early in 1687 and joined the Tres
Marías group in September (Ducéré, *Corsaires*, 179). Subsequent
Spanish accounts estimate the pirates' strength at from eighty to more
than 100 men.

103 Olea, *"Historia de Mazatlán,"* 25. This contradicts frequent
statements of de Lussan, who claimed that French pirates respected
the churches. Maybe there were a few English in this group.

the port and took several prisoners, offering to exchange them for forty cows.[104]

When the viceroy received word of these raids he commissioned a fleet of three vessels, with 207 men, to capture the buccaneers. This squadron sailed from Acapulco on November 15, 1687, and returned early the following January without having accomplished anything. Since it was not known that the sailing of the eastbound Manila galleon had again been postponed, two of the same ships then went out to protect that vessel. They got only as far as Cape Corrientes, returning to Acapulco February 13.[105]

In June, 1688, the buccaneers crossed to La Paz bay in Lower California where they spent three months careening their ships. On November 14 of that year a major attack was made on the town of Acaponeta. According to the Spanish report, some eighty to ninety men landed from a medium-sized ship, a *balandra,* and a launch, and marched ten leagues inland to the town. They killed several people and retired with prisoners and booty to the amount of twenty *cargas* (burro-loads) of silver. Among the prisoners were forty women and two priests. The pirates then went into hiding on the nearby island of Palmito, after setting the hostages' ransom at 100,000 pesos.[106]

Again the viceroy ordered out his defense force,

---

104 Robles, *Diario,* II, p. 150.

105 *Ibid.,* 153, 155. *México* 57, AGI.

106 Robles, *Diario,* II, p. 167. *México* 58, AGI. Ducéré, *Corsaires,* 181-182.

this time a single warship with 143 men commanded by General Antonio de Mendoza. Leaving
Acapulco on December 17, they passed one of the
Manila ships, the "Nuestra Señora del Pilar,"
which reported that a second and larger galleon
was following. Eight days out of Matanchel, on
January 23, 1689, Mendoza came up to the pirate
ship. There was a battle at close quarters lasting
from 9 a.m. until 2 p.m., after which the Spaniards
chased the buccaneers for two days until they were
lost to sight. Mendoza then went in to Matanchel
and Navidad, where he met the second galleon,
"Santo Christo de Burgos," just arrived from
Manila. Although Mendoza heard that the pirates
were hiding out in the Tres Marías, he elected to
escort the galleon to Acapulco, where they arrived
February 15.[107]

Meanwhile the buccaneers landed near Rosario
and left word that all their prisoners would be put
to the sword unless ransom was paid at once. Early
in May, 1689, a pathetic letter reached Guadalajara from Padre Aguilar, one of the prisoners. The
pirates had sliced off his ears and nose, and the
wretched priest begged that his captors be given
what they wanted: money and tobacco.[108] Other
Spaniards who had been detained in the Tres
Marías managed to escape to the woods, build a

---

107 *Ibid.* The pirate account says the 22-gun Spanish warship fled
after the battle, in which the French lost two dead and eighteen
wounded.

108 Robles, *op. cit.*, II, pp. 179, 181.

192 PIRATES OF NEW SPAIN'S WEST COAST

boat, and get across to Chamela. One of them had been a prisoner for a year and eight months. According to his testimony the buccaneers numbered ninety-two men and had a small ship fitted with eight guns, and a large twenty-four-oar canoe. They told him they had been sent out by the king of France, and he overheard them say that they planned to go back to Peru and then cross to the Philippines.[109] It would seem that the pirates concentrated their activities in a relatively small district opposite the Tres Marías. The bishop of Guadalajara wrote in mid-1689 that their raids had devastated the provinces of Acaponeta and Senticpac, which "are now almost ruined, although before they were very prosperous," and that they had done much damage in the mining camp of Rosario.[110]

In May, 1689, the Frenchmen sailed from the coast of Acaponeta leaving behind all their prisoners with the exception of three men, one of them a Franciscan priest. Whether they received the ransom demanded, we do not know. Later in the same month they visited Salagua, where the Franciscan and one other prisoner were released.[111]

Again the viceroy's fleet set out from Acapulco, on July 18, 1689. Now there was a squadron of three ships manned by 327 soldiers and sailors

[109] *México* 58, AGI.
[110] *Guadalajara* 61, AGI.
[111] Robles, *op. cit.*, II, p. 181. *México* 58, AGI.

under General Andrés de Arriola. Their orders
were to capture the pirates at all costs. They called
at Salagua and Navidad, were off Cape Corrientes
on August 18, entered Banderas Bay, and proceeded to the Tres Marías Islands. Here they spent
three days in a close examination of the harbors,
but their quarry had disappeared. At Matanchel,
on August 24, Arriola heard that the pirates had
been seen off the Yaqui River earlier in the month,
and soon afterward had crossed to La Paz, in
Lower California. The Spanish fleet continued
northward, arriving off the Yaqui toward the
middle of September. There they were caught in
a hurricane and blown back to the Sinaloa River.
Apparently Arriola decided not to follow the
pirates to California. He returned south, calling
once more at the Tres Marías in late October and
reaching Acapulco on November 20. He was of
the opinion that the enemy already had departed
for Peru.[112] The Manila galleon reached Acapulco,
seemingly without escort, December 19, 1689.[113]

Little is known about the further activities of
the Tres Marías buccaneers. They were too weak
to attempt the capture of the Manila galleon.
There was not much else to plunder, and they had
no desire to fight the Spanish fleet now that they
were so few and alone in a hostile sea. Quite possibly they went to Lower California to careen their

[112] *Ibid.*
[113] *México* 59, AGI.

ship before retiring southward.[114] Early in 1691 some fishermen visited the Tres Marías and found the remains of a shipyard and a cache of provisions left behind by the pirates, which may indicate that they sailed directly from La Paz, unwilling to risk another visit to their old base.[115] It would appear that they left Mexican waters in early 1690 and cruised south to Juan Fernández Island where they divided the loot, which came to eight or nine thousand pesos per man. Then they crossed to Peru and took several prizes, one with a considerable amount of gold and silver.[116] In attempting to return to the Atlantic they were shipwrecked in the Straits of Magellan, lost most of their treasure, and spent ten cold months building boats from the wreckage. The survivors, less than twenty buccaneers, somehow managed to reach the West Indies, probably in 1692.[117]

---

[114] The Jesuit P. Sigismundo Taraval, writing probably in the 1740s, says that Pichilingue Island (near La Paz) was so named after a pirate who "years ago, before the conquest" careened his ship there (Taraval MS.). The conquest referred to is that of California by the Jesuits, from 1697.

[115] Letter from viceroy, April 1, 1691, in *México* 60, AGI.

[116] Froger, *Relation d'un voyage*, 107. Froger says the pirates had been seven years in the Pacific when they reached Juan Fernández. Cf. Funnell, *Voyage Round the World*, 20-21. Burney, *Chronological History*, IV, pp. 333-334, mentions that the English Captain Strong, off Guayaquil on August 21, 1690, "learnt here that a French privateer had within the last six weeks done much mischief on the coast."

[117] Burney, *op. cit.*, IV, p. 295. Froger, *op. cit.*, 108, says they reached Cayenne, and implies that one of their group, Macerty, returned to France sometime before 1695 and furnished the information used by Froger.

V
English Privateers and Smugglers

English Privateers and Smugglers

After the Treaty of Ratisbon in 1684, the Caribbean buccaneers found it increasingly difficult to carry on their nefarious profession. The gallows now awaited them in many ports where once they were welcome to revictual and dispose of their loot. However, Europe was entering a confused period of alliances and wars which enabled some pirates to continue their activities as legitimate privateers. Before the end of 1688 the Dutchman William of Orange was sharing the throne of England, and Spain's traditional enemies, Holland and England, were allied with her against France. For several years beleaguered France was unable to send privateers to the Pacific, but this did not discourage a company of English merchants from dispatching Captain John Strong to the South Sea with the pretext of cruising against the French. Strong had a well-armed ship and a good store of merchandise for contraband trade with the Spanish colonies. He entered the Pacific through the Straits of Magellan in May, 1690, and succeeded in disposing of most of his cargo in Peru and Ecuador, although he met with a hostile reception in some ports. To his surprise, Strong heard that there really was a French ship cruising in the Pacific (she was the tiny vessel of the Tres Marías pirates, on their way home). He returned to the Atlantic at the end of 1690.[1]

In New Spain steps were taken at last to provide a permanent defense fleet for the Pacific coast. Two small galleys or galiots were built at Realejo for the exclusive purpose of protecting Mexican ports and shipping from piratical attacks. The flagship had the breath-taking name of "Jesús Nazareno Santo Domingo y San Gaspar." The smaller "Nuestra Señora de la Soledad y San Francisco de Paula" had a keel of 33½ *codos* (46 feet), twenty-eight oars, and a normal complement of fifty soldiers in addition to the rowers. The armament of these vessels must have been quite small, probably a few light swivel guns, but their maneuverability would make them useful in a hit-and-run engagement. The first of the galiots reached Acapulco in December, 1690, and the second in March, 1691. For the next few years they patrolled the coast from Guatulco to Lower California, investigating rumors of pirates and serving as convoys to the Manila galleon.[2]

The latter ship was now better prepared to defend herself. She carried ten to thirty heavy guns and a number of perriers, which were taken up out of the hold and mounted when the coast of

[1] Burney, *Chronological History*, IV, pp. 329-336.
[2] Letters from viceroy: April 1, 1691, in *México 60*, AGI; November 20, 1695, in *México 62*, AGI.

Upper California came into view on the eastbound sailing. However the old order to keep well out to sea until approaching Acapulco was not being complied with in the 1690's. During these years the Manila ship normally sighted Cape San Lucas before crossing the mouth of the gulf to Cape Corrientes. One or both of the coastguard galiots waited for her at either of these capes and escorted her into Acapulco.[3] A report of pirates on the coast of Peru caused the viceroy to send out both galiots, their crews augmented with fifty soldiers of the palace guard, to meet the Manila ship in the fall of 1692. No trace was seen of the pirates nor of the galleon, which had in fact been wrecked on her westbound voyage.[4]

In November and December of 1694 some ships thought to be pirates were reported off Salagua, Acapulco, and the coast of Soconusco (southern Chiapas). Once again the viceroy sent out his galiots, one of which cruised as far as the Tres Marías Islands. The strange vessels were later identified as three cacao ships from Peru accompanied by the Manila galleon herself, the latter having bypassed Acapulco to illegally sell her cargo in Peru.[5]

Toward the end of King William's War, in

---

[3] Letter from viceroy, August 6, 1692, in *México* 471, AGI. Churchill, *Voyages*, IV, pp. 472-474.

[4] Robles, *Diario*, II, p. 267. Letter from viceroy, August 6, 1692, in *México* 471, AGI.

[5] Robles, *Diario*, II, p. 314; III, pp. 9-12. Letter from viceroy, November 20, 1695, in *México* 62, AGI.

June, 1695, the French at last prepared their long-expected assault on the Spanish Pacific. A powerful squadron of six vessels commanded by M. de Gennes sailed from la Rochelle with the intention of raiding Spanish ports and shipping in the South Sea. However, the expedition came to nought. De Gennes found the weather so bad in the Straits of Magellan that he gave up and returned to the Atlantic in the spring of 1696.[6]

The Treaty of Ryswick in 1697 put an end to hostilities between Spain and France. The following year the French Compagnie Royale de la Mer du Sud fitted out two fifty-gun ships and some smaller vessels for a contraband trading voyage to South America. Command of the expedition was entrusted to a naval officer, M. de Beauchesne Gouin. The two larger ships reached the Pacific through the Straits of Magellan in January, 1700, and proceeded up the coast to Valdivia, but they were driven off by Spanish cannon. When the viceroy of Peru heard of the intruders he sent out a squadron from Callao to repel them, although Beauchesne Gouin was able to sell his cargo at Arica and Ilo before taking refuge in the Galápagos Islands in June, 1700. He returned to the Atlantic in January of the following year.[7]

During the War of the Spanish Succession, from

---

[6] Froger, *Relation d'un voyage*, 1-113. Burney, *Chronological History*, IV, *pp*. 339-342.

[7] Burney, *op. cit.*, IV, pp. 375-382. Fernández Duro, *Armada Española*, V, p. 306.

1702 to 1713, Spain was blockaded by the English and could no longer communicate with her oversea possessions. For the duration of the war, and indeed for some years afterward, Spain's new ally France took over the profitable business of trading with the Spanish American colonies. There were perhaps ten to twenty French ships each year on the west coast of Peru, some of which reached the Pacific shores of New Spain. Although these could hardly be called pirate expeditions, or even contraband voyages except in a legalistic sense, some mention will be made below of those French vessels which called at Mexican Pacific ports during this period.[8]

William Dampier, the son of a moderately prosperous farmer, was born in the county of Somerset in 1652. He went to sea at the age of seventeen, fought in the Dutch Wars, helped manage a Jamaica plantation, took a turn at logwood cutting in Campeche, and became a pirate probably in 1676. For the next thirty-four years he cruised about the world, much of the time as an ordinary seaman, doing his share of the drudgery and fighting, and employing his spare moments in keeping up a most fascinating journal. Dampier's writings are an entertaining mixture of observations about the places he visited, the winds and the tides, plant

[8] Fernández Duro, *op. cit.*, VI, p. 92. Zaragoza, *Piraterías de los ingleses,* 183.

and animal life, and a thousand details of genuine scientific value and great human interest. He seems to have been a thoroughly intelligent and likable fellow and a rather gentle buccaneer.

Largely on the strength of the published account of his adventures with Sharp, Davis, Swan, and other pirates, Dampier was given command of an expedition sent out to explore Australia in 1699. The voyage was a failure, and on his return to England Dampier was courtmartialed and declared incompetent to command a ship. The accusation was not entirely unjust. No doubt Dampier was a skilled pilot and navigator, but his lack of success as a leader of men can only partly be attributed to bad luck. However, in 1703 England was at war with both Spain and France, and in spite of his recent misfortune Dampier was given command of the privateer "Saint George," with a commission from the Lord High Admiral "to proceed in a War-like manner" against the enemy in the Pacific.

The "Saint George" had been fitted out by a company of London merchant-adventurers. She carried twenty-six guns and a crew of 120. The men received no wages but were merely promised a share of the plunder, the usual procedure among pirates but an unsatisfactory arrangement for a privateer, especially an unsuccessful one. Dampier sailed from Ireland in September, 1703, in the company of a ninety-ton galley, "Cinque-ports," with sixteen guns and sixty-three men. The commander of "Cinque-ports," Charles Pickering, died in Brazil, and his place was taken by the first officer, Thomas Stradling. The two vessels entered the Pacific separately around Cape Horn in January, 1704, and rendezvoused at Juan Fernández the following month. From there they crossed to the Peruvian coast and took a few prizes, arriving in the Gulf of Panamá early in May. After a thwarted attempt to raid the gold mines at Santa María, the two privateers cruised in the gulf and captured a large Spanish vessel loaded with provisions. They dropped anchor off the old pirate base of Taboga Island on May 25, 1704.[9]

Here Dampier and Stradling had an argument and parted ways. The "Cinque-ports" returned to Juan Fernández, cruised for a time off Peru, and foundered near Gorgona Island early the following year. Stradling and seven other survivors were taken prisoners by the Spaniards.[10]

Dampier, in the "Saint George," also cruised south from Panamá, took a few prizes off Ecuador, and had an inconclusive engagement with a Spanish warship on August 2. Nine days later he sailed from Atacames in the company of a ten-ton prize renamed "Dragon," and set his course for the Gulf of Nicoya, where the two ships dropped anchor on August 27. While the "Saint George" was being refitted at one of the islands in the gulf, the "Dragon" captured a forty-ton bark loaded with

[9] Funnell, *Voyage Round the World,* 1-46.
[10] Burney, *op. cit.,* IV, pp. 447-448.

sugar, wine, and brandy. In order to lighten the "Saint George" for careening, her ammunition and stores were transferred to the new prize bark. At this point Dampier's chief mate, John Clipperton, took possession of the loaded prize and deserted with twenty-one men. He was considerate enough to put ashore part of the ammunition and supplies before sailing out of the gulf on September 13.[11] Subsequently Clipperton took two prizes in the harbor of Realejo. He returned to Nicoya to careen his vessel, probably in November, 1704, and then sailed westward across the Pacific to China and back to Europe.[12]

Dampier was now left with only sixty-four men in the worm-eaten "Saint George" and the tiny "Dragon." In spite of his weak condition he determined to cruise northward for the Manila galleon, and the two vessels sailed out of Nicoya on October 4, 1704. Off Guatemala on the twentieth they captured an eighty-ton bark en route from Zihuatanejo to Realejo. The prize had nothing of value except a few provisions. On November 22 the privateers ran in to Zihuatanejo, where they had a brief skirmish with a party of Spaniards. Here they took on sixteen sacks of flour, filled their

---

[11] Funnell, op. cit., 47-68.

[12] Ibid., 295-296. Burney, op. cit., IV, p. 447. It was probably on this voyage that Clipperton discovered the island which bears his name, a small atoll 670 miles southwest of Cape Corrientes, very close to the westbound track of the Manila galleon.

water casks, and rummaged the little fishing village before sailing away on November 29.[13]

Dampier's next port of call was the deserted bay of Maruata, about one hundred miles southeast of Salagua, where he arrived on December 3. There he lay several days while his men took on water and wood and caught turtles in the estuary. Leaving Maruata in the evening of December 7, the "Saint George" overhauled a sixty-ton pearling bark on her way from Lower California to Acapulco. The prize was in ballast, but the Englishmen relieved her crew of a few pearls. They continued northward, reaching Navidad Bay on December 15, where they seized a newly-built vessel of fifty tons which had been sent out to meet the Manila ship. This prize was loaded with food and a good supply of powder and shot, most of which was jettisoned by her crew. From Navidad the two privateers and one of their recent prizes sailed out past Chamela in search of the Manila ship which was due to arrive.[14]

In the morning of December 17, 1704, not far from Chamela, Dampier and his two consorts finally sighted and bore down on the great Manila galleon "Nuestra Señora del Rosario y San Vicente Ferrer," lumbering southward on the final stage of her long voyage to Acapulco. For more than a century these ships had made their

---

13 Funnell, *op. cit.*, 75-79.
14 *Ibid.*, 80-83.

annual crossing unmolested, and apparently the "Rosario's" officers had not been warned of the presence of an enemy. Consequently the privateers were able to run by at close range and deliver several broadsides while the Spaniards were scrambling about attempting to clear their guns. However, Dampier hesitated to grapple and board the huge vessel, and while he was arguing the point with his unruly crew the "Rosario" started firing into his ship with devastating effect. Funnell, the English chronicler, claims that the "Saint George" had only five-pound shot, which did little damage to the stout galleon, while the "Rosario's" eighteen- and twenty-four-pound shot crashed through the privateer's decaying timbers. One of these landed "between Wind and Water in our Powder Room; by which we had two foot of Plank driven in on each side the Stem." The crippled privateers gave up the fight, and were in fact lucky to get off without being sunk or captured.[15]

Dampier's men, disgusted at losing the great prize which had been their goal since entering the Pacific, were now in a thoroughly mutinous mood. They blamed their failure on their commander's lack of resolution, although it is hard to see how such a small crew could have succeeded in taking the "Rosario," with several hundred armed men aboard, even if they had been able to grapple her. The "Saint George" was now in very bad condition and provisions were short. One of the prizes

[15] *Ibid.,* 83-84. *México* 1330; *Filipinas* 207; AGI.

was abandoned, apparently the "Dragon." It would seem that the pearling vessel was retained and accompanied the "Saint George," hugging the coast, past Acapulco and Guatulco, reaching Amapala Bay on February 6, 1705.[16]

At Amapala, Dampier was deserted by William Funnell and the majority of his men, thirty-five in all, who took the prize bark and armed her with four of the "Saint George's" guns. Funnell sailed out of Amapala on February 12 and headed westward across the Pacific to Indonesia, where his ship was seized by the Dutch.[17]

Dampier stayed a few days longer at Amapala trying to patch up his wretched "Saint George." He was now left with only twenty-eight men and boys, all of his officers and the more experienced seamen having gone off in the various mutinies. He sailed from Amapala sometime in February, 1705, and made his way south to Ecuador. The diminutive crew made a successful raid on the island village of Puná, and captured a small bark off the rock of Lobos de la Mar on the Peruvian coast. Dampier and his men moved over to the prize and left their rotten "Saint George" to sink. From Peru they crossed to the East Indies and, like Funnell, had their ship confiscated by the Dutch. Dampier at last arrived in England in 1707, in time to embark on still another voyage around the world.[18]

16 Funnell, *op. cit.*, 84-86.
17 *Ibid.*, 86-223.
18 Burney, *op. cit.*, IV, pp. 443-444.

The frustrated attempt on the Manila galleon caused general rejoicing in New Spain, but it was clear that further attacks by the English were likely as long as the war lasted. The viceroy strengthened Acapulco's defenses, had sentinels stationed all along the Pacific shore, and reiterated the order to maintain the coastal area for several leagues inland free of settlements and cattle. In September, 1707, a report reached Mexico that twenty-two English vessels had entered the Pacific after taking on supplies at Buenos Aires. More soldiers and cannon were sent to Acapulco, but the two coastguard galiots apparently had been lost as there was no vessel available to escort the Manila ship.[19] The latter arrived at Navidad Bay on January 20, 1708, at the same time that four enemy ships were reported seen at Boca de Apisa, just south of Colima. The galleon lay over at Navidad and Salagua until additional soldiers from Guadalajara could be taken aboard, after which she continued unmolested to Acapulco.[20] In all likelihood the "enemy" ships were contraband traders. In April the viceroy wrote that the rumor of twenty-two privateers had proved to be false.[21]

A French captain by the name of Nicolas de Frondat, made an unusual trading voyage across the northern Pacific following the track of the

---

[19] *México* 481, AGI.

[20] Correspondence with the *alcaldes mayores* of Autlán and Colima, in *Filipinas* 204, AGI.

[21] Letter, April 11, 1708, in *México* 481, AGI.

Manila galleons, in the summer of 1709. His ship, "Saint-Antoine," sailed from China in February of that year, touched at Lower California, and reached Banderas Bay on August 21. According to the viceroy's report the vessel carried sixty guns and a crew of 150. Frondat attempted to trade some of his cargo for beef cattle at Banderas, but he found the countryside barren of provisions. Eventually the "Saint-Antoine" disposed of most of her merchandise in Peru and Chile, and returned to France with almost £2,000,000.[22]

Meanwhile another privateering expedition to the Pacific was being prepared in England, largely at the instance of Dampier. A group of Bristol merchants provided financial support and equipped two vessels under the command of Woodes Rogers, a highly competent officer and navigator. The flagship "Duke" was of 320 tons and mounted thirty-six cannon. Her consort was the "Duchess," 260 tons and twenty-six guns, commanded by Stephen Courtney. Each ship had a second captain, Dr. Thomas Dover on the "Duke" and Edward Cooke on the "Duchess." William Dampier accompanied the expedition as "Pilot for the South-Seas." The crews totaled 333 men, many of them landsmen and foreigners (mostly Dutch), who were to receive wages in addition to shares in

[22] Burney, *op. cit.*, IV, pp. 487-488. Letter from viceroy, October 31, 1709, in *México* 482, AGI. Dahlgren, *Voyages français*, 470-71.

the booty. Another innovation, reminiscent of the Pechelingue expeditions a century earlier, was a council composed of the principal officers and presided by Dr. Dover, which was to meet whenever an important decision had to be made. Because of the personalities involved, this curb on Rogers' authority proved to be a mistake and almost brought the expedition to disaster. Rogers held the usual commission from the Lord High Admiral to wage war against both French and Spaniards.[23]

The two ships hoisted anchor at Cork in September, 1708, and entered the Pacific around Cape Horn in January of the following year. After a rendezvous at Juan Fernández Island (where they picked up Alexander Selkirk, who had been marooned by Stradling four years before), they cruised along the coasts of Chile and Peru taking a good number of prizes, many of them French vessels. They occupied and looted the city of Guayaquil from May 5 to 17, 1709.[24] The viceroy of Peru sent out a punitive squadron of five ships under Admiral Don Pedro de Alzamora Ursino, who went all the way to New Spain and return without meeting the enemy.[25]

Toward the end of September, 1709, the privateers sailed from the Galápagos Islands, their

---

[23] The authorities on this expedition are Rogers, *Cruising Voyage,* and Cooke, *Voyage to the South Sea,* both first-hand accounts.

[24] Rogers, *op. cit.,* 123-193.

[25] Fernández Duro, *Armada Española,* VI, p. 93. Zaragoza, *Piraterías de los ingleses,* 182.

course set for New Spain. At this time the squadron had been augmented by two prizes: the "Marquis," formerly the French "Havre de Grace," fitted with twenty guns and commanded by Edward Cooke; and a small bark commanded by Henry Duck. Rogers' cruise in South America had been the most successful one in many years. He had accumulated booty to the value of £20,000 in gold, silver, and precious stones, with another £60,000 worth of goods. The ships' complements had largely escaped the ravages of scurvy and had had few casualties from fighting. By now the crews were well disciplined and practiced in gunnery and in the tactics of grappling and boarding. Only recently the ships had been cleaned, trimmed, and provisioned, and their arrival on the west coast of Mexico was well timed to coincide with that of the Manila galleon, their next objective.[26]

Word of Rogers' depredations in Peru reached Mexico City in September, 1709, only a few weeks before his arrival off Colima. Again the garrison of Acapulco was alerted and strengthened, and valiant efforts were made to warn the Manila ships. Two galleons were expected from the Orient in the winter of 1709-10, the recently built "Nuestra Señora de Begoña" of 900 tons, and "Nuestra Señora de la Encarnación y del Desengaño," of about 400 tons burden. There was no ship in Acapulco to be sent out, but the viceroy commanded that all available vessels on the west

26 Rogers, *op. cit.*, 215-242. Cooke, *op. cit.*, 311.

coast were to proceed at once to Cape San Lucas, or if they were unable to get that far, to the Tres Marías Islands. The boat used by the Jesuits to supply their missions in Lower California went out from Matanchel, its crew reinforced with soldiers, to meet the China ships. A few pearling vessels were commandeered for the same purpose. Apparently none of these ships succeeded in getting across the gulf.[27]

Meanwhile Rogers, with the "Duke" and "Duchess," came up to Cape Corrientes on October 12 followed by the prize barks two days later. Dampier had suggested a rendezvous at the Tres Marías Islands, and there the squadron lay from mid-October until November 4, taking on water and wood and securing some game and fish. On November 12 they were off Cape San Lucas. The "Duke," "Duchess," and "Marquis" spread out for a distance of twenty leagues off the cape, while the smaller bark cruised about between them and acted as messenger.[28] On November 28 the bark went in to San Lucas Bay for water and was met by a swarm of naked Indians. The Jesuits had not yet extended their missions to the tip of Cal-

---

[27] Letter from viceroy, October 31, 1709, in *México* 482, AGI. Tonnage of the galleons is according to Rogers and may be exaggerated. In 1702 a royal cédula raised the limit of the Manila trade to 300,000 pesos eastbound and 600,000 pesos westbound, to be carried in two ships of not more than 500 tons each. (*Filipinas* 932, AGI). The value of the cargoes was still greatly increased by contraband, and the ships were usually overloaded, but the legal tonnage was probably adhered to.

[28] Rogers, *op. cit.*, 266-280. Cooke, *op. cit.*, 332-335.

ifornia, nor were they to do so for another twenty
years. Some of the bark's crew went ashore to the
Indian rancheria, a collection of little open huts,
where they were hospitably received and given a
meal of broiled fish.[29]

As the weeks went by the English began to
think that the galleons had eluded them, or that
perhaps their sailing had been canceled. On the
last day of 1709 the privateer council met and
decided to abandon the blockade and retire to the
coast before starting across the Pacific. Accordingly the fleet went in to San Lucas and prepared
to sail the following day. However, the "Duke"
remained close off the cape, and at nine in the
morning of January 1, 1710, the watcher at her
masthead caught sight of a sail which proved to
be the smaller of the two galleons, "La Encarnación." Rogers took after her, followed by the
"Duchess," and chased her all night. Early next
morning he came within range of the galleon and
started firing his bow chasers, being answered by
the stern perriers of the "Encarnación." The galleon, commanded by a Frenchman, Jean Presberty,
had twenty cannon and the same number of perriers, against thirty-six guns on the "Duke." A
running fight ensued with frequent broadsides
from both ships, until the "Encarnación" struck
her colors. The "Duchess" came up somewhat
tardily and fired on the Spaniards after they had
surrendered. The battle had lasted several hours,

[29] Rogers, *op. cit.*, 284-286. Cooke, *op. cit.*, 336.

but neither ship was severely damaged. The Spaniards, however, had lost some twenty-five dead of the 193 crew and passengers. The only serious casualty on the "Duke" was Rogers himself, who had a chunk of his upper jaw torn off by a musket shot.[30]

The following day, January 3, the English took their prize into San Lucas Bay. The value of the galleon's cargo was estimated at 2,000,000 pesos, although much of it was of a perishable nature. When it was learned that a second and richer galleon was coming up, the privateer council met and decided to send out the "Duchess" and "Marquis" to intercept her, overruling Rogers who wanted to use all three ships. While his consorts were cruising off the cape Rogers moved the prisoners into the prize bark and repaired the damage on the "Duke" and the "Encarnación." [31]

On January 4 or 5 the second of the galleons, "Nuestra Señora de Begoña," came into sight. She was much larger than the "Encarnación," with an armament of forty guns and forty perriers and about 350 men aboard. However her commander, Fernando de Angulo, points out that he had only thirty soldiers fit for combat, most of the others being down with scurvy after the long crossing. The "Duchess" overtook the second galleon in the late afternoon and engaged her with a

---

[30] Rogers, op. cit., 291-294. Cooke, op. cit., 363. Fernández Duro, op. cit., VI, p. 94. Filipinas 207, AGI.

[31] Rogers, op. cit., 295.

few broadsides, receiving somewhat more than she gave. The next day Rogers, who had seen the action from shore, came up in the "Duke," having left some of his men to guard the prisoners. It is not clear how long the engagement lasted, but eventually the three English vessels were beaten off, badly damaged, and retired to San Lucas Bay. The English had thirty-four killed and wounded in this battle. Spanish casualties on the "Begoña," which reached Acapulco also in a battered condition, were eight dead and several injured.[32]

On January 12, 1710, Presberty and the rest of Rogers' prisoners sailed for Acapulco in the privateer bark which they had been obliged to purchase with a letter of credit payable in London. The English generously let them keep the clothes on their backs and a few personal possessions. Meanwhile the galleon "Encarnación" was rebaptized "Batchelor" and Dr. Dover was put in command. Several more days were consumed at San Lucas repairing the damage on the four vessels, attending to the wounded, and taking on wood and water. Finally on January 21 the squadron hoisted anchor and started its long voyage across the Pacific. Rogers arrived in England in October, 1711. The gross profits of his cruise were estimated at £170,000.[33]

---

[32] *Ibid.,* 296-300. Fernández Duro, *op. cit.,* 94-95. Filipinas 207, AGI. Rogers intimates that the battle lasted several days, while the Spanish version says the action began on January 4 and ended the following morning.

[33] Rogers, *op. cit.,* 305-312. Cooke, *op. cit.,* 446.

The comparative success of Rogers' voyage around the world was not soon to be repeated, although the menace of privateers continued to plague New Spain for some years more. The Manila galleon "Nuestra Señora del Rosario" was loaded with silver and ready to sail from Acapulco in March, 1711, when a message arrived from Guadalajara that three enemy ships had been seen near Senticpac on February 21. The viceroy ordered a delay in the galleon's departure until the rumor could be investigated, but by the time his courier reached Acapulco the "Rosario" had sailed. It would seem that this was another illusion, or perhaps a matter of contraband, as no more was heard of the "pirates." [34] In November, 1712, two French merchant vessels from China made calls at Banderas Bay. Then, early in February, 1713, a French trader came up from Peru and dropped anchor in Puerto Marqués, the contraband haven adjacent to Acapulco. The viceroy was cautious in his report to the king about this visit, but it appears that a certain amount of merchandise was exchanged for "supplies." The Frenchman remained in port almost two months before returning south. [35]

In July, 1713, the War of the Spanish Succession finally came to an end when the Treaty of Utrecht was signed. By its terms the English were com-

---

[34] Letter from viceroy, October 31, 1711, in *Filipinas* 119, AGI.

[35] *Idem*, March 9, 1716, in *México* 1327, AGI. Dahlgren, *Voyages français*, 480-84.

missioned to supply Spanish America with 4,800 Negro slaves each year, and furthermore they received the privilege of introducing five hundred tons of merchandise annually, free of duty, to the Spanish Atlantic ports. In fact this limit was not adhered to, and after 1713 commerce with Vera Cruz and Porto Belo was almost a monopoly of the English merchant-traders. At first the French continued to dominate trade on the Pacific side of America, but after 1716 their ships were no longer officially welcome in Peru and New Spain. Gradually the Spaniards reestablished their trading monopoly with the west coast, for the first time sending cargoes directly from Spain around Cape Horn to Peru and Mexico (after 1718).[36]

Before the news of the war's end reached America there was a final brief invasion of English privateers in the Pacific. Three or four enemy ships came up around South America early in 1713. One of them was commanded by a Captain Charpes,[37] who took two prize vessels at Paita and looted the town. From Peru he ran across to the Galápagos Islands and continued on to the Gulf

---

[36] Priestley, *José de Gálvez,* 23, 30. Zaragoza, *Piraterías de los ingleses,* 191-198, 219-220. The French continued to trade on the coasts of Chile and Peru, and occasionally as far as New Spain, until 1724 and even later, but subject to the same risk of confiscation and imprisonment as other foreigners. Burney, *op. cit.,* IV, p. 512, says fourteen French trading ships arrived in the Pacific in 1721. Haring, *Spanish Empire,* 337, says that it was not until 1740 that Spanish ships began to sail around the Horn.

[37] The name is probably misspelled; the only source we have seen for this cruise is a Spanish one (*Filipinas* 119, AGI).

of Panamá. Using the old pirate base of Taboga Island, he captured five more Spanish ships. In September, 1713, he was reported to be careening his ships at Cocos Island. One of his prisoners later declared that the pirate crew was composed of forty-eight Irishmen and twenty Negroes. From Cocos, Charpes seems to have sailed northwest to the vicinity of Guatulco, where three enemy ships were seen early in November. The viceroy of New Spain sent out the usual warnings, and the Manila ship arrived safely in February, 1714.[38]

Another enemy squadron, or perhaps the same one, arrived in Banderas Bay probably in June, 1714. It consisted of two vessels, one a large ship which had been taken as a prize off Huanchaco (in Peru), the other first described as an English privateer, *"fragata de guerra de yngleses corsarios."* They came in under a French flag, but it developed that they were contraband English traders. The authorities in Guadalajara sent a company of soldiers down to the bay, but their commander promptly made friends with the intruders and bought a few trinkets himself. Finally an *oider* of the *audiencia* of Guadalajara, Antonio del Real y Quesada, went down to the coast and confiscated both ships and cargoes, imprisoning the crews.[39]

---

[38] *Filipinas* 119, AGI.

[39] Letter of June 18, 1714, in *Guadalajara* 77, AGI. One of the privateer captains taken at this time may have been John Clipperton (see footnote 40, below).

The following year, 1715, two more English ships, frankly pirates, came up around Cape Horn. One of them, the "Prince Eugene," was probably commanded by John Clipperton, who had sailed with Dampier in 1703-04. Arriving off Paita they seized two Spanish vessels with merchandise valued at 400,000 pesos. The viceroy of Peru dispatched a forty-gun warship which overtook and captured one of the pirates in the Gulf of Panamá, recovering the loot and carrying off the crew to be hanged at Lima. The other pirate ship, the "Prince Eugene," in the company of a prize vessel, fled northward, and both were in turn captured by a Spanish warship sent out by the *audiencia* of Guadalajara early in 1716.[40]

On the death of Louis XIV in 1715, Felipe V of Spain announced his claim to the throne of France. The result was another war, in which France, Holland, and England were allied against Spain. Once again English privateers prowled the seas for Spanish treasure, with the approval and support of their government. As far as we know, only one privateer expedition was sent out to the Pacific

[40] Fernández Duro, *Armada Española*, VI, p. 128. Zaragoza, *op. cit.*, 190-191. Letter from viceroy, March 20, 1716, in *México* 1327, AGI. No mention by name of Clipperton appears in these sources, but Betagh, *Voyage Round the World*, 127, identifies "Prince Eugene" as "the same ship in which Captain *Clipperton* was circumvented and taken in his late voyage in [the Pacific]." On the other hand, a royal cédula of 1719 states that "Lord Cliperton" was captured in Banderas Bay in 1714 (*Guadalajara* 76, AGI). Whenever it was, he appears to have been soon released and returned to England in time to leave on another cruise in February, 1719.

during this war, which ended in 1720. It consisted of two ships fitted out by a group of merchant-adventurers. The "Success," commanded by John Clipperton, had thirty-six guns and 180 men at the start of her voyage. Clipperton had made two previous cruises in the Pacific, the first when he served as Dampier's mate and deserted, and the second as an independent pirate when he was captured by the Spaniards (see above, and notes 39 and 40). The "Speedwel," with twenty-four guns and an original crew of 106, was commanded by a naval lieutenant, George Shelvocke. The second captain or chief mate on the "Speedwel" was Simon Hatley, or Hately, who had been with Dampier in 1703-05 and also on Woodes Rogers' cruise in 1708-11. Both Shelvocke and Clipperton were of a temperamental nature and did not get along well with each other nor with their men. Clipperton spent most of the time drunk in his cabin, while Shelvocke was a martinet without the means to enforce discipline. It was intended that they cruise together, but a week after leaving Plymouth in February, 1719, they separated and did not see each other again until two years later.[41]

Clipperton entered the Pacific through the Straits of Magellan at the end of August, 1719,

---

[41] The two primary sources for these voyages are Shelvocke and Betagh. The latter was captain of marines on the "Speedwel" and was taken prisoner by the Spaniards in March, 1720. He describes the cruise of the "Success" using the journal of Clipperton's mate, George Taylor.

and reached Juan Fernández Island three weeks later. By this time thirty of his men had died from scurvy and exposure. After a month spent careening and refitting, the "Success" crossed to the mainland and took several prizes on the coast of Peru. One of them, a seventy-ton bark renamed "Chichly," was fitted out as an additional privateer with eight guns and a crew of twenty-three under the command of a Captain Mitchell. The "Chichly" sailed northward in December, 1719, was seen in the vicinity of Nicoya, and then disappeared.[42] Meanwhile Clipperton ran out to the Galápagos Islands in January, 1720, to avoid contact with a Spanish fleet of three warships commanded by Don Bartolomé de Undinzu. On February 1, just north of the Galápagos, he captured the "Prince Eugene," the same vessel which had been taken from him on his previous cruise. Aboard was the Marquis of Villa-Rocha and his family on their way to Lima. Accompanied by this prize, and perhaps by another, Clipperton then steered for "Port Velas," probably Culebra Bay at the western extremity of the Nicoya peninsula, where he arrived on March 19, 1720. By now

---

[42] According to Shelvocke, *op. cit.*, 316, Clipperton ordered Mitchell "to go to some island on the coast of Mexico" and wait for him there. Subsequently Clipperton was unable to find the island referred to. When he called at Port Velas he heard that Mitchell had been there before him, but did not see him again. Perhaps the island was the atoll of Clipperton (see footnote 12, above), which could have been used as a base for attacking the westbound Manila galleon.

Clipperton's force had been reduced to some eighty-five men and boys.[43]

At "Velas" the prize "Prince Eugene" was released, and the Marquis's wife and child were put ashore while ransom could be secured for the Marquis, who remained aboard as a hostage. On April 20 the "Success" sailed northward, and on May 1 reached Amapala Bay, where she lay among the islands for three weeks waiting in vain for the promised ransom. From Amapala Clipperton returned south to Peru and Chile, taking more prizes and rummaging the coastal towns. In November he had a brief encounter with the Spanish warships from which the "Success" emerged unscathed, although one of the prizes was recaptured. In December Clipperton was back at the Galápagos, and from December 29, 1720, until January 31, 1721, he lay at Cocos Island, taking on fish, wood, and water. A shack was set up on the beach to shelter the large number of scurvy invalids in the crew. Eleven men, three English and eight Negroes, were left behind on Cocos Island (according to Clipperton they had deserted). From Cocos, the "Success" ran across to the Veragua mainland, where she came up off Coiba Island and met George Shelvocke and the forty surviving members of his crew, on February 5, 1721.[44]

---

[43] Betagh, *Voyage Round the World*, 87-128. Zaragoza, *op. cit.*, 202-203.

[44] Betagh, *op. cit.*, 129-147.

Shelvocke had entered the Pacific in October, 1719, cruised up the coast of Chile, called at Juan Fernández, and returned to Peru in February, 1720. He completely lost control of his men, some of whom deserted to the Spaniards. Among the latter were the second captain Hatley and the chronicler Betagh. On June 5, 1720, the "Speed-wel" was driven ashore and wrecked on Juan Fernández Island. With great difficulty Shelvocke induced his men to build a sort of pinnace, and got away from the island on October 17. The following month he captured a 200-ton vessel, "Jesús María," at Pisco, and transferred his men and stores to the prize. Paita was occupied by the privateers for a day early in December, 1720, and a few more prizes were taken and released. Leaving Gorgona Island on December 13, Shelvocke's men, who were now operating their ship by majority rule, tried to steer westward across the Pacific, but they could make no headway against the contrary winds. On January 24, 1721, they dropped anchor at Coiba Island, still uninhabited and an excellent base. After making a few foraging raids on the mainland they were cruising out from Coiba when, as has been mentioned, they met Clipperton on February 5.[45]

With only about 120 men between them it was logical, even imperative, for Clipperton and Shelvocke to join forces. The "Jesús María" had

---

[45] Shelvocke, *Voyage Round the World*, 162-315.

accumulated much loot but was low on supplies, while the "Success" had a fair store of provisions but little plunder. The Manila galleon, "Santo Christo de Burgos," was at the moment preparing to sail from Acapulco with several million pesos in silver. The Spaniards knew that privateers were in the vicinity and had taken the usual precautions, but a quick cruise up the coast and a bold attack by the two ships as the galleon came away from land might have met with success. At this crucial point Clipperton and Shelvocke quarreled again and parted company, although they took the same course northward. They separated near Caño Island, sighted each other near Acajutla, and came within hailing distance off Guatulco and Puerto Angel. The two privateers arrived off Acapulco on March 23, their captains finally agreeing to attempt the capture of the Manila ship together. However the inconstant Clipperton soon decided to abandon this project and try to take the galleon by himself off the Philippines. During the night of March 28, about a week before the galleon actually sailed out, the "Success" deserted Shelvocke and started across the Pacific, reaching Guam two months later. In China, Clipperton's crew deserted and his vessel was condemned. Eventually he reached Europe in a Dutch ship, in 1722, and died a few days afterward.[46]

Meanwhile Shelvocke, badly in need of food

---

[46] *Ibid.*, 315-333. Betagh, *op. cit.*, 149-151.

and water, returned southward. On April 11 he took a 300-ton ship, "La Sacra Familia," off Acajutla. The prize had six guns and was a better vessel than the "Jesús María," so Shelvocke moved into her and left his old ship behind. While at Acajutla the English were informed that war was at an end, and consequently they were now considered pirates. The *alcalde mayor* of Sonsonate tried to induce them to surrender, but the terms were not attractive and Shelvocke and his men sailed for Panamá. Their water supply was very low and none was found in a two-day search at Amapala Bay. The chronicler assures us that for some days they were reduced to drinking their urine, but at last they found water at Caño Island on May 6. Six days later they arrived off Coiba Island, where they took on more water and wood.[47]

Now the privateer-pirates, weary of their interminable cruise, thought of surrendering to the Spaniards after all. On May 26 they took a bark loaded with provisions out of Chiriquí, whose captain agreed to pilot them into Panamá. Five days later they captured another prize, a ship which had been sent out to pursue them, but meanwhile the Spaniards had massacred the prize crew on the Chiriquí bark and escaped overboard. Having only thirty-odd men and more than eighty prisoners, Shelvocke released the latter in the two prizes after taking their supplies and guns aboard

---

[47] Shelvocke, *op. cit.*, 334-363.

the "Sacra Familia." With a well-armed ship and plenty of provisions, together with considerable hard-earned loot, the English began to reconsider their position. They discarded their plans of surrender and decided to return home across the Pacific, although for some reason Shelvocke insisted on running all the way to Lower California for careening. They made another brief call for water at Caño Island, passed Cape Corrientes early in August, and spent three days in the Tres Marías Islands, before reaching Cape San Lucas on August 22.[48]

Shelvocke remained a week at San Lucas trimming and cleaning his ship and taking on wood and water for the long crossing. Relations between the privateersmen and the primitive California Indians seem to have been unusually cordial. On August 29, 1721, the "Sacra Familia" hoisted anchor and set sail for China, with only thirty white men and a few Negroes, reaching Macao toward the end of the year. There Shelvocke sold his ship and returned to London in an East Indiaman, arriving in August, 1722. Subsequently he was tried for piracy and for embezzling much of the plunder, but he escaped to Holland.[49]

[48] *Ibid.*, 365-399.
[49] *Ibid.*, 401-409.

VI
The Last Pirates

The Last Pirates

Spain and her colonies enjoyed a long period of peace following King Philip's War. Jacob Roggewein, a Dutchman sent out by the West India Company on an exploring trip, barely touched in Chile in March, 1722.[1] A new viceroy on his way to Peru in 1724 found an armed English ship riding in Panamá harbor with the specious pretext of stopping contraband slave shipments. Suspecting that the real mission of this warship was to chart the coast, the viceroy had her cannon impounded.[2] At the same time a strong and temporarily successful effort was made to discourage foreign contraband on the Pacific side of America. A few French ships were confiscated, and of three Dutch traders who called at Peru in 1726, two were seized by the Spaniards and the third fled back to the Atlantic.[3] Still another Dutchman, known to the Spaniards as Cornelio Andrés, was driven from the coast of Peru in 1735, but managed to sell part of his cargo at Panamá and Realejo before crossing to the Moluccas.[4]

[1] Burney, *Chronological History*, IV, pp. 556-557.
[2] Zaragoza, *Piraterías de los ingleses*, 211-219.
[3] *Ibid.*, 225-226. Fernández Duro, *Armada Española*, VI, p. 187.
[4] Zaragoza, *op. cit.*, 227.

In 1739, war – the War of Jenkins' Ear – broke out again between England and Spain. This conflict was largely the result of abuse of the trading privileges with Spanish America, which the English obtained after the War of the Spanish Succession. Months before the declaration of hostilities, the British Admiralty began preparing a series of naval expeditions to prey on Spanish shipping in Europe, America, and the Far East. The squadron in which we are interested was ordered to raid the west coast of South America, destroy as many Spanish ships as possible, and above all seize the Manila galleon. Its commodore was George Anson, one of the most competent officers in the Royal Navy. Anson was forty-two years old at the start of the cruise. He was a professional seaman, experienced in naval warfare, a disciplinarian, and an extremely aloof and taciturn personality.[5]

Anson's fleet, when it sailed from England in September, 1740, consisted of five men-of-war, a sloop, and two victualers, with a total complement of more than fifteen hundred men and boys, and an armament of 236 guns. Anson had a most unfortunate passage around Cape Horn, in which

---

[5] Three first-hand English accounts have been used of Anson's cruise: Walter, *Voyage round the world,* was written by Anson's chaplain on the "Centurion." The others are Thomas, *True and impartial journal,* and [Anon.], *Voyage to the South Seas.* The abridged (1947) edition of Walter has been used for the first part of the cruise up to the arrival at Coiba Island; thereafter all three sources are followed, using the original (1748) edition of Walter.

his ships and men were badly punished by the
Antarctic gales. The crews were made up largely
of invalids to start with, men who had been taken
out of old seamen's homes and hospitals, together
with lads who had never used a musket nor been
to sea. Two of the larger ships turned back to the
Atlantic and a third was wrecked on the coast of
Chile. When the remaining vessels rendezvoused
at Juan Fernández Island, nine months after their
departure, they mustered only 340 men, less than
half the original complements. Most of the survivors were disabled with scurvy. At this time the
fleet consisted of the flagship "Centurion," sixty
guns, commanded by Anson; the "Gloucester,"
fifty guns, Captain Mathew Mitchel; the sloop
"Tryal," eight guns, Captain Charles Saunders;
and the store ship "Anna," eight guns, Captain
Gerard. While at Juan Fernández, the "Anna"
was broken up and her crew and stores taken
aboard the other ships.[6]

The Spaniards had intelligence of Anson's cruise
before he sailed from England, and had fitted out
a powerful squadron in Spain to intercept him.
The Spanish fleet, however, had been wrecked in
the South Atlantic, with the result that Anson was
not to encounter a single warship to oppose his
designs on Peru and New Spain. Furthermore it
had been so long since his departure from England that it was assumed his squadron had been

---

[6] Walter (1947), 1-109.

lost, and the viceroy of Peru had recently lifted the embargo he had imposed on Pacific shipping.[7]

Anson remained three months at Juan Fernández, giving his sick time to recuperate and repairing the damage to his ships. The squadron sailed in September, 1741, and took two large prizes off Valparaíso, which were promptly converted into British warships. The first ship was "Nuestra Señora de Carmelo," of 450 tons, now commanded by Lieutenant Philip Saumarez, and the second, the "Arranzazu," of 600 tons, was given to Captain Saunders in place of his sloop, the "Tryal." The latter was in such poor condition that she was scuttled. In November two more merchant ships were captured on the coast of Peru, after which Anson determined to raid the port of Paita, where he heard there was a considerable treasure. That place was taken almost without resistance, looted, and burned on November 24-27. On leaving Paita, Anson scuttled five ships in the harbor and took off a sixth, "La Soledad." [8]

The next objective of the squadron was the Manila galleon. After sinking three of their prizes, the English sailed northward from Peru late in November, bound for Coiba Island, where they rendezvoused toward the middle of the following month. The fleet was now composed of the "Centurion," "Gloucester," "Arranzazu," "Carmelo,"

---

[7] *Ibid.*, 25-37, 108.
[8] *Ibid.*, 110-129.

and a fifth prize, "Nuestra Señora del Carmen," of 270 tons. During their cruise in South America they had taken eleven Spanish vessels, destroyed a large amount of valuable merchandise at Paita, and acquired loot to the value of some £55,000, mostly in silver coin.

Anson spent only three days at Coiba, taking on wood and water and trimming his ships. He sailed on December 19, 1741, and the next day took a small bark, the "Jesús Nazareno," out of Panamá, bound for Chiriquí with a cargo of oakum and salt. This prize was scuttled and her crew taken prisoner. Then the squadron ran into a frustrating alternation of northwest gales and dead calms which kept it from making any headway, at a time when Anson was extremely interested in getting north to intercept the Manila ship. Cocos Island was seen in the distance early in January, 1742, and remained in sight for five days. Finally a good wind came up and carried them northward, and on the night of February 9 a light was seen, which proved to be the volcano of Colima. The squadron now ran eastward along the coast toward Acapulco, passing Zihuatanejo on February 24. One of the ships' boats was sent on ahead and entered the mouth of Acapulco harbor in the night of February 27-28. The boat's crew captured three fishermen and returned with them to the flagship where Anson questioned the prisoners and learned, to his great disappointment, that the

Manila galleon had arrived in port on January 20, only a few weeks before his squadron had come up.[9]

In Acapulco the Spaniards had been expecting Anson for months, having received full details of his exploits in Peru. The castle of San Diego recently had been repaired and now had thirty-one brass and cast-iron cannon, the largest using twenty-five-pound shot. Its normal garrison of eighty-six men had been reinforced with more than five hundred Spanish and Creole soldiers from the interior, in addition to the three militia companies. The galleon which had just arrived in port was a small one, "Nuestra Señora del Pilar." One of Anson's boats had been seen on the coast west of Acapulco, and the viceroy determined to postpone the westward sailing of the galleon until the danger had passed.[10]

Hoping that his presence was not yet known to the Spaniards, and that the galleon, loaded with silver, would sail in a few days for Manila, Anson came up off Acapulco on March 12, with his squadron of five ships. He disposed them in a half-circle off the port, out of sight of land but close enough to each other (three leagues apart) so that the galleon could not slip by unobserved. This

---

[9] Walter (1748), 214-250. Thomas, *op. cit.*, 100-110. Anon., *op. cit.*, 260-269.

[10] Villaseñor, *Theatro Americano*, I, pp. 186-188. Thomas, *op. cit.*, 106-107, mentions that a barge had gone in close to shore and had seen (and presumably been seen by) a man on the beach.

blockade was kept up until April 4, when a council was held aboard the "Centurion." By this time Anson was convinced that he had been discovered and that the galleon would not sail until late in the year, which proved to be the case. The thought of entering Acapulco and trying to seize the treasure was considered, and discarded as impractical. Of more immediate importance, the ships' dwindling water supply had to be replenished. Consequently the squadron was ordered to give up the blockade and run up the coast to Zihuatanejo, where they arrived April 18, 1742. Meanwhile Lieutenant Hughes and six men were left to cruise off Acapulco in a cutter.[11]

Anson and his men lay three weeks in the deserted bay of Zihuatanejo, during which time the "Centurion" was heeled and her bottom cleaned and pitched. On April 19 a landing party went eighteen miles inland and met only a solitary rider, who escaped them. There were other enemies nearby, however. Anson's French cook wandered off a short distance and was taken prisoner. On April 30 Lieutenant Brett was sent with two boats to nearby Petatlán Bay, where he found a large body (English estimates vary from 140 to 200) of armed enemy horsemen waiting on the beach. However, they fled when the English fired on them. Meanwhile the ships were being watered

[11] Walter (1748), 250-258. Thomas, *op. cit.*, 110-114. Anon., *op. cit.*, 276-278.

and trimmed, the gunpowder was taken ashore to dry, and the men fished and shot pheasants and iguanas. Anson determined to destroy his prizes, as he did not have enough men to take them across the Pacific. Just before sailing he had them towed ashore, scuttled, and burned.[12]

On May 8 or 9, the "Centurion" and the "Gloucester" sailed from Zihuatanejo toward Acapulco in search of the cutter which had been left to cruise off the port, but it was nowhere to be found. After several days Anson assumed that Lieutenant Hughes and the others had fallen into the hands of the enemy, and he sent ashore a letter to the *castellano* offering to exchange the fifty-eight prisoners he had aboard for the seven men of his cutter. However, while he waited for an answer, on May 16 the cutter appeared and its men were taken aboard, more dead than alive, having been driven some eighty leagues eastward. Unable to land through the heavy surf, they had been six weeks at sea in their twenty-foot open boat, subsisting on sea turtles and rain water.[13]

There was no further incentive for Anson to remain on the Mexican coast, and he prepared to

[12] Walter (1748), 258-272. Thomas, *op. cit.*, 114-117, 121. Anon., *op. cit.*, 278-281.

[13] Walter (1748), 272-277. Thomas, *op. cit.*, 122. Anon., *op. cit.*, 281-283. Letter from viceroy, October 6, 1742, in *México* 1256, AGI. The English sources agree on the details of Hughes' adventure. However the viceroy states that the cutter's crew were taken prisoners and exchanged for the 58 Spanish captives.

sail for China. The prisoners were given two prize launches in which to find their way ashore, and on May 17 or 18, 1742, Anson's squadron left Acapulco behind and began to cross the Pacific.[14]

Where Anson failed in New Spain, he was tremendously successful in the Philippines. After a series of misfortunes, including the loss of the "Gloucester" and a good part of the crews, the English captured the westbound galleon "Nuestra Señora de Covadonga" on July 1, 1743, off Cape Espíritu Santo. Her loss, with some 1,500,000 pesos in silver, was a crippling blow to the merchants of Manila. Anson's "Centurion" reached England in June, 1744, almost four years after her departure, with the great Spanish treasure in her hold. Eventually Anson became First Lord of the Admiralty and introduced many reforms in the Royal Navy. He died in 1762.[15]

It must be admitted that ending this study with Anson's voyage is a bit arbitrary. Spain was at war on several occasions between 1742 and the consummation of Mexican and Central American independence, and enemy privateers occasionally carried these wars into the Pacific, although few of

---

[14] Walter (1748), 278. Thomas, *op. cit.,* 122. Anon., *op. cit.,* 283.

[15] *Filipinas* 121 and 256, AGI. The "Nuestra Señora del Pilar," which was in Acapulco during Anson's blockade, sailed on December 7, 1742, with 1,300,000 pesos on the register and reached Manila safely in March, 1743. The "Covadonga" crossed eastbound in 1742-43 and left Acapulco on April 15, 1743, with 1,200,000 registered pesos.

them got as far north as Mexico. Two Dutch
traders crossed from China to New Spain in 1746-
47 and met with a cold reception at Matanchel and
Navidad.[16] After 1750, smuggling became both
more international and more widespread. Toward
the end of the eighteenth century and the beginning of the next, the west coast ports of America
were more and more frequented by contraband
traders from England, France, Holland, and
finally the United States. More often than not
these visitors were amicably received in defiance
of the prohibition of trade with foreigners, but
inevitably some smugglers ran afoul of the law, or
of venal and grasping Spanish officials. Ships were
seized, shots exchanged, ports raided, and people
killed much as in the days of the buccaneers.

During and after the Wars of Independence,
Admiral Thomas Cochrane's squadron, presumably in the service of the republican government
of Chile, committed all kinds of atrocities with the
pretext of combating the royalists. Some of their
raids on the Mexican west coast, particularly the
looting of Lower Californian ports in 1822, can
best be described as vicious piratical forays. For
the remainder of the nineteenth century, and again
during the Mexican revolution of 1910-1920, the
tranquil life in the few Pacific coast ports was
occasionally disturbed by hostile landings and

---

[16] Gerhard, "Dutch Trade Mission."

bombardments. More recently still, the term "pirate" has been applied by Mexican and Central American writers to foreign fishing boats operating off their coasts. To some extent the application is appropriate. In the 1920s some of these interlopers had special shot made for their harpoon guns, and more than one Mexican coastguard launch was sent to the bottom with all hands.

CONCLUSION

During the 167 years (1575-1742) to which this study has been limited, available records indicate that at least twenty-five armed expeditions of foreign interlopers, ranging in size from one to eleven vessels, reached the Pacific shores of Central America or Mexico. Of them, twelve were English, five Dutch, four French, and four of mixed or doubtful nationality. Usually their arrival in these waters was the final stage of a cruise up the west coast of South America, although four expeditions reached New Spain after crossing the north Pacific, and four were composed entirely or in part of buccaneers who marched overland from the Caribbean. Of the twenty-five, seven were armed contraband traders, nine were privateers or ships of war, and nine were unlawful pirate cruises.

Comparative estimates of loot taken and damage

done to the Spanish colonies are difficult to arrive at, but the following table will give an idea of the relative success of the more important expeditions.

Expedition	Prizes taken [17]	Plunder[18]	Comments
Oxenham (1576)	(2)	Nil	Captured by Spaniards
Drake (1579)	3	Slight	Rich prize in Peru
Cavendish (1587)	6	Large	Took Manila galleon
de Lint (1600)	2	Slight	
Speilbergen (1615)	1	Slight	Defeated Spanish fleet in Peru
Schapenham (1624)	0	Nil	
Morgan (1671)	5	Large	Sacked Panamá
Sharp et al. (1680-81)	14	Large	More loot in Peru
Buccaneers (1684-90)	18	Large	
Dampier (1704)	7	Slight	Repulsed by Manila galleon
Rogers (1709-10)	1	Large	Took Manila galleon
Charpes (1713)	5	?	
Clipperton (1715?)	0	Nil	Captured by Spaniards
Shelvocke (1721)	3	Slight	More loot in Peru
Anson (1741-42)	1	Nil	Took Manila galleon in Philippines

[17] Between the Gulf of Panamá and California.
[18] Relative quantity, between the Gulf of Panamá and California.

Piracy on the Pacific side of America never reached the proportions that it assumed in the Caribbean. The difficulties of getting there and returning, and the problems of securing provisions, were often overwhelming. Furthermore, the west coast of Central America and Mexico was not a very profitable cruising ground for pirates or privateers, unless they were fortunate and strong enough to take a silver shipment from Peru, or a Manila galleon. The Pacific coast of South America was somewhat more accessible and had more local shipping and coastal towns with a certain amount of wealth.

Although a cruise on the west coast of New Spain was often an unprofitable venture for pirates, their raids caused the Spaniards a great deal of inconvenience and financial loss. Loot taken away was only a small part of the damage. The value to Spain of the ships sunk, towns burned, agriculture and commerce destroyed and inhibited, and other direct and indirect effects of these raids ascended to many millions of pesos. While it is true that relatively little was done to fortify Pacific ports or protect shipping, still the threat of aggression caused the Spaniards to go to considerable trouble and expense. Whenever word arrived of the presence of a foreign enemy in the Pacific, although the alarm often proved to be false, the placid life of the viceroyalty was replaced by turmoil. Soldiers had to be equipped and provisioned and sent down to the coast, and ships fitted out and sent off on always hazardous and costly voyages. Construction of the original castle at Acapulco cost 142,000 pesos, and the maintenance of permanent garrisons there and elsewhere along the coast was a constant drain on the royal revenues. The fortifications at Panamá, and the maintenance of an armada for convoying silver shipments from Peru, resulted in another heavy expense to the crown. One reason for the inflated prices of Chinese goods and the consequent high cost of living in New Spain and Peru was the potential danger of an enemy attack on the Manila galleon.

Perhaps the most permanent effect of piracy on the west coast of Mexico was an indirect one brought about by the reiterated order forbidding or discouraging colonization of the coastal region. The long stretches of deserted seashore, including much fertile territory which still lies untilled and abandoned, may well be partly the result of this old colonial policy intended to discourage pirate visits.

Glossary and Bibliography

Glossary

ADMIRAL. 1. The flagship of a fleet. Equivalent to Spanish *capitana*. 2. Commander of a fleet.

ADVENTURER. A shareholder in a commercial, privateering, or pirate expedition.

ALCALDE MAYOR. In New Spain, a local royal official roughly corresponding to the English mayor of a city, but often having jurisdiction over a large territory.

ALMIRANTA. A ship carrying the second-in-command of a Spanish fleet, or the smaller of two ships. Equivalent to English *vice-admiral*.

ARMADA. A fleet of warships.

AUDIENCIA. A tribunal which, in Spanish America, acted as a governing body over a territory which might include several kingdoms and many provinces. It was composed of a president and several *oidores*.

BAJEL. A small ship, or large boat.

BALANDRA. A small sailing vessel, usually with one deck and a single mast. Roughly equivalent to English *bilander*.

BARGE. A ship's boat, equipped with oars.

BARK. A small sailing vessel.

BOW CHASER. A small cannon, usually mounted on a swivel, installed in the bow of a ship. See *perrier*.

BUCCANEER. An independent pirate or freebooter in America operating outside the law. The buccaneer originated in the Caribbean and spread to the Pacific. *Cf. pirate* and *privateer*.

CABALLERO. 1. A Spanish nobleman. 2. A raised portion, or bastion, inside or on the perimeter of a fort.

CAPITANA. The flagship of a Spanish fleet, equivalent to English *admiral*.

CARGA. A burro-load.

CASTELLANO. The commanding officer in a Spanish fortress; the chief royal official in Acapulco.

CÉDULA. Short for *real cédula*. A general communication or letter from the king of Spain.

CODO. Linear measure equivalent (in New Spain) to 16½ English inches. The *codo real* or *codo de ribera* used in Spain was longer, 23.37 inches.

CORREGIDOR. Similar to *Alcalde mayor, q. v.*

CUTTER. A small sailboat.

ENCOMENDERO. A Spanish settler, often a conquistador, whom the king had appointed patron of the Indians within a specified area. The encomendero was supposed to Christianize and "defend" the Indians, in return for which he received their tribute and labor.

ENSENADA. Cove or bay.

ESTANCIA. A farm or cattle ranch.

EXPEDIENTE. Collection of documents relating to a specific incident or case.

FERIA. A trade fair, specifically that held in Acapulco on the arrival of the Manila galleon, usually in January or February.

GALIOT. A small galley, often without a deck. Equivalent to Spanish *galeota*.

GALLEON. Equivalent to Spanish *nao, navío,* rarely *galeón*. A large sailing vessel, commonly with three masts and two or more decks. The type of Spanish galleon used in the Pacific had a comparatively wide beam, a low waist, and a high poop and forecastle. However, according to a report from the viceroy of New Spain in 1602, the Manila galleons at that time had a proportionally narrower beam than those in the Atlantic, while the ships built in Peru were the narrowest of all (letter, March 8, 1602, in *México* 25, AGI). The largest galleons in the Pacific were those used in the Manila-Acapulco trade, from 200 to 1,000 tons burden. A royal cédula of 1726 gives the following specifications for building Manila galleons: Keel, 60 *codos* (presumably these are Spanish *codos de ribera,* in which case the equivalent would be 116 ft. 10 in.). Beam *(manga),* 20 *codos* (39 ft.). Depth from the top of the keel to the lower surface of the first deck, 10 *codos* (19 ft. 6 in.). The width of the poop *(yugo)* was to be two-thirds that of the beam. The hull at the point where it began tapering to form the bow *(mura)* should be ½ *codo* (11½ in.) wider than at the beam *(manga).* The crew was to consist of ten officers and 250 men. *(Real cédula,* October 31, 1726, in *Guadalajara* 78, AGI).

GALLEY. Equivalent to Spanish *galera.* A proportionally long, shallow-draft vessel with a single covered deck, propelled by oars and often by sails as well. Her advantage over other ships lay in her greater speed and maneuverability, but she was likely to founder in a heavy sea.

GENTILHOMBRE. A Spanish royal courier with official dispatches.

GROMMET. An apprentice seaman, or ship's boy. Spanish *grumete.*

GUN. Cannon, or great gun.

HARQUEBUS. An awkward hand weapon firing a single bullet. It was usually fired from the shoulder without support, but sometimes a fork rest was used. It was replaced by the more reliable if heavier musket, *q.v.*

JACHT (Dutch). A small, light pursuit ship. Roughly equivalent to English *pinnace,* Spanish *patache.*

LAUNCH. A large ship's boat.

LEAGUE. Vague linear measure varying from 2½ to 3 English miles or more. Theoretically it was the distance which could be traveled on foot in an hour. At sea a league was three nautical miles.

LONGBOAT. A large open ship's boat, narrow in the beam, normally propelled by oars but often having a movable mast and sail. It might carry as many as sixty or seventy men.

MESTIZO. A person of mixed Spanish and Indian blood.

MULATTO. A person of mixed Spanish and Negro blood.

MUSKET. A heavy individual weapon about 5 or 6 feet long, using a double iron bullet. It had to be aimed and fired with the aid of a fork rest. It was deadlier and more accurate than the harquebus.

NORTH SEA. The north Atlantic Ocean, including the Caribbean and the Gulf of Mexico.

OIDOR. One of the judges or governing officials in an *audiencia (q. v.)*

PECHELINGUE. (From the Dutch port of Flushing or Vlissingen; variant spellings, Pichilingue, Pechelinga, etc.). Term applied by the Spaniards to the Dutch pirates and privateers of the 16th and 17th centuries, and sometimes by extension to pirates of other nationalities.

PERRIER. (Variant spellings, perier, petrero, patararo, canon perier, etc., Spanish *pedrero.)* A small, breech-loading, swivel cannon, of either cast-iron or brass, which originally fired a stone ball. Later it used iron shot. It was often kept in the bow or stern of a ship. The perrier's main value was in repelling boarders and for close action in general.

PESO. Equivalent to *piece of eight.* The basic silver coin of Spanish America, slightly larger than a U.S. silver dollar.

PILOT. (Spanish *piloto,* or *piloto mayor).* The officer in charge of navigation on a Spanish ship. The captain or general of a Spanish ship was usually a temporary royal appointee who did not interfere in nautical matters.

PINNACE. A small ship, light and narrow, propelled by both sail and oars. Often it was used as a dispatch boat or tender of a larger ship.

PIRAGUA. A long, flat-bottomed, dugout canoe, widened by cutting the log in two and inserting planks. Fernández Duro *(Armada Española, v, p. 181)* gives the dimensions of a piragua which must have been unusually large: 90 ft. long, 16-18 ft. wide in the center, with two masts, 44 oars, and room for 120 men. However, the Spanish foot was only eleven English inches long, which gives a length of 83 feet and a width of 14½ to 16½ English feet. It carried a cannon in the bow and four perriers in the stern. Yet it only drew 1½ ft. fully loaded.

PIRATE. A sea robber, specifically one who attacked Spanish American ports and shipping in peacetime. When war was declared, he became a *privateer*. Occasionally the pirates traveled overland and raided towns far in the interior.

PLATE. Silver, usually in bars but sometimes in coin.

PRESIDENT. Spanish *presidente*. The presiding officer of an *audiencia (q. v.)* In Panamá and Guatemala the president was also governor and captain general. In Mexico he was the viceroy of New Spain.

PRIVATEER. Spanish *corsario*. 1. A privately owned ship sent to cruise against the enemy in wartime. 2. Officer or crew member of such a ship.

PRIZE. A captured ship.

REAL DE MINAS. A town with silver or gold mines in the vicinity.

RUMMAGE. To pillage, or scour the countryside for loot or provisions.

SOUTH SEA. The Pacific Ocean.

STERN CHASER. A small cannon, usually mounted on a swivel, in the stern of a ship. See *perrier*.

TAMEME. An Indian burden carrier in New Spain.

VICE-ADMIRAL. A ship carrying the second-in-command of a fleet. Equivalent to Spanish *almiranta*.

Bibliography

MANUSCRIPT SOURCES

Archivo General de Indias, Sevilla (AGI). Ramos: Audiencia de Filipinas; Audiencia de Guadalajara; Audiencia de México; Patronato Real

[Carbonel, Esteban]. "Relación del biaxe a la California Hecho por el capn. Francisco de Horttega." Ayer Collection, Newberry Library, Chicago

Sluiter, Engel. "The Dutch on the Pacific Coast of America, 1598-1621." Ph.D. thesis, University of California, Berkeley, 1937

[Taraval, Sigismundo]. History of the Pericu rebellion, without title. Ayer Collection, Newberry Library, Chicago

PUBLISHED SOURCES

Alessio Robles, Vito. Acapulco en la historia y en la leyenda. 2d ed. México, 1948

[Anonymous]. An Historical Account of the Circumnavigation of the Globe, and of the Progress of Discovery in the Pacific Ocean, from the Voyage of Magellan to the Death of Cook. New York, Harper and Brothers, 1837

[Anonymous]. A voyage to the South Seas, and to many other parts of the world, performed from September 1740 to June 1744, by Commodore Anson. London, 1745

Artíñano y de Galdácano, Gervasio de. Historia del Comercio con las Indias durante el Dominio de los Austrias. Barcelona, 1917

Ayres, Philip, ed. The voyages and adventures of Capt. Barth. Sharp and others, in the South Sea: being a journal of the same. London, 1684

Bancroft, Hubert Howe. History of Central America. San Francisco, 1883-1887. 3 vols.

———. History of Mexico. San Francisco, 1883-1888. 6 vols.

———. The New Pacific. New York, 1912

Betagh, William. A Voyage Round the World. Being an Account of a Remarkable Enterprize, begun in the Year 1719, chiefly to cruise on the Spaniards in the great South Ocean. London, 1728

Borah, Woodrow. Early Colonial Trade and Navigation Between Mexico and Peru. (Ibero-Americana: 38). Berkeley and Los Angeles, 1954

Brand, Donald D. "The development of Pacific coast ports during the Spanish colonial period in Mexico," 577-591 in Estudios antropológicos publicados en homenaje al doctor Manuel Gamio. Mexico, 1956

Burgoa, Francisco de. Geográfica descripción. México, 1934. 2 vols.

Burney, James. A Chronological History of the Discoveries in the South Sea or Pacific Ocean. London, 1803-1817. 5 vols. Note: Vol. IV contains "History of the Buccaneers of America," which has been published separately in various editions.

Calderón Quijano, José Antonio. Historia de las fortificaciones en Nueva España. Sevilla, 1953

[Callander, John]. Terra Australis Cognita: or, Voyages to the Terra Australis, or Southern Hemisphere. Edinburgh, 1766-1768. 3 vols.

Cavo, Andrés. Historia de México. México, 1949

[Churchill]. A collection of Voyages and Travels. London, 1732. 6 vols.

Clavigero, Francisco Javier. The History of [Lower] California. Translated from the Italian and edited by Sara E. Lake and A. A. Gray. Stanford University and London, 1937

Colección de "Cuadros Sinópticos" de los pueblos, haciendas y ranchos del Estado Libre y Soberano de Oaxaca. Oaxaca, 1883

Colección de documentos inéditos, relativos el descubrimiento, conquista y organización de las antiguas posesiones españolas en América y Oceanía. Madrid, 1864-1884. 42 vols.

Colección de libros y documentos referentes á la historia de América, tomo viii, Relaciones históricas y geográficas de América Central. Madrid, 1908

Cooke, Edward. A voyage to the South Sea and round the world. London, 1712

Corbett, Julian S. Drake and the Tudor Navy. London, New York, Bombay, 1899. 2 vols.

Dahlgren, M.E.W. Voyages français á destination de la mer du sud avant Bougainville. Paris, 1907

Dampier, William. A New Voyage Round the World. London, Argonaut Press, 1927

Dictionary of National Biography, vol. iii. London, 1921-1922

Ducéré, E. Les corsaires sous l'ancien régime. Bayonne, 1895

Esquemeling, John. The Buccaneers of America. London, George Allen and Unwin, 1951. Note: There are several translations and many editions, some much better than others. The original (Dutch) edition is Alexandre Olivier Exquemelin, De Americaensche Zee-Rovers (Amsterdam, 1678). For Ringrose's journal, the Broadway Translations edition (London and New York, n. d.) has been used.

Fernández Duro, Cesareo. Armada Española desde la unión de los reinos de Castilla y León. Madrid, 1895-1903. 9 vols.

Froger, le Sieur. Relation d'un voyage fait en 1695, 1696, & 1697 aux Côtes d'Afrique, Détroit de Magellan, Brézil, Cayenne & Isles Antilles, par une Escadre des Vaisseaux du Roy, commandée par M. de Gennes. Paris, 1698

Funnell, William. A Voyage Round the World. Containing an Account of Captain Dampier's Expedition into the South-Seas in the Ship St George, in the years 1703 and 1704. London, 1707

[Gage, Thomas]. Thomas Gage's Travels in the New World, J. Eric S. Thompson, ed. Norman (Oklahoma), 1958

Gay, José Antonio. Historia de Oaxaca. 2d ed. Oaxaca, 1933. 2 vols.

Gemelli Carreri, Juan F. Viaje a la Nueva España. México, 1955. 2 vols.

Gerhard, Peter. "A Dutch Trade Mission to New Spain, 1746-1747," Pacific Historical Review, XXIII (1954), 221-226

———. "Pearl Diving in Lower California, 1533-1830," Pacific Historical Review, XXV (1956), 239-249.

———. "The Tres Marías Pirates," Pacific Historical Review, XXVII (1958), 239-244

Gobernantes del Perú – cartas y papeles siglo XVI. Madrid, 1921-1926. 14 vols.

Guijo, Gregorio M. de. Diario, 1648-1664. México, 1952. 2 vols.

Hakluyt, Richard. The Principal Navigations, Voiages, Traffiques and Discoveries of the English Nation. 2d ed. London, 1598-1600. 3 vols.

———. Voyages & Documents selected with an introduction and a glossary by Janet Hampden. London, 1958

Haring, Clarence Henry. The Buccaneers in the West Indies in the XVII Century. New York, 1910

———. The Spanish Empire in America. 3d printing, New York, 1957

[Hawkins, Richard]. The Observations of Sir Richard Hawkins, Knt, in his Voyage into the South Sea in the Year 1593. C. R. Drinkwater Bethune, ed. London, Hakluyt Society, 1847

Hydrographic Office, Pub. no. 84. Sailing Directions for the West Coasts of Mexico and Central America. 9th ed. Washington, 1951

Kelly, I. T. Excavations at Chametla, Sinaloa. (Ibero-Americana: 14). Berkeley, 1938

[Lebrón de Quiñones, Lorenzo]. Relación Breve y Sumaria de la Visita Hecha por el Lic. Lebrón de Quiñones, Oidor del Nuevo Reino de Galicia, por Mandado de su Alteza. Guadalajara, 1956

Lussan, Raveneau de. Journal du voyage fait a la mer de sud, avec les flibustiers de l'amerique en 1684. & années suivantes. Paris, 1689. Note: Except where "1689" is indicated, a modern translation has been used: Marguerite Eyer Wilbur, transl. and ed., Raveneau de Lussan Buccaneer of the Spanish Main. Cleveland, 1929

Madariaga, Salvador de. The Fall of the Spanish American Empire. New York, 1947

Masefield, John. On the Spanish Main. New York, 1906

Means, Philip Ainsworth. The Spanish Main. New York and London, 1935

Mota y Escobar, Alonso de la. Descripción geográfica de los reinos de Nueva Galicia, Nueva Vizcaya y Nuevo León. 2d ed. México, 1940

Murguía y Galardi, José María. "Estadística antigua y moderna de la Provincia, hoy Estado libre, soberano é independiente de Guajaca," Boletín de la Sociedad Mexicana de Geografía y Estadística, VII (1859), 161-196

Nuttall, Zelia, ed. New Light on Drake. A Collection of Documents Relating to His Voyage of Circumnavigation 1577-1580. London, Hakluyt Society, 1914

Ocaranza, Fernando. Crónicas y Relaciones del Occidente de México, Tomo I. México, 1937

Olea, Héctor R. "Historia del puerto de San Juan Bautista de Mazatlán," Noroeste, II, núm. 16 (México, 1952), 25-32

Orozco y Berra, Manuel. Apéndice al Diccionario Universal de Historia y de Geografía. México, 1855-1856. 3 vols.

———. Historia de la Dominación Española en México. México, 1938. 3 vols.

Paso y Trancoso, Francisco del, ed. Epistolario de Nueva España. México, 1939-1942. 16 vols.

Paso y Trancoso, Francisco del, ed. Papeles de Nueva España. 2a serie. Madrid, 1905-1906. 6 vols.

Peralta, Manuel María de. Costa-Rica Nicaragua y Panamá en el siglo xvi su historia y sus límites. Madrid and Paris, 1883

——. Costa-Rica y Colombia de 1573 á 1881. Madrid and Paris, 1886

Portillo y Díez de Sollano, Alvaro del. Descubrimientos y exploraciones en las costas de California. Madrid, 1947

Power, R. H. "Portus Novae Albionis Rediscovered?," Pacific Discovery, VII (1954), 10-12

Pretty, Francis. "The Admirable and Prosperous Voyage of the Worshipfull Master Thomas Candish," in Richard Hakluyt , The Principal Navigations, III. London, 1600

Priestley, Herbert Ingram. José de Gálvez, visitor-general of New Spain (1765-1771). Berkeley, 1916

Robles, Antonio de. Diario de Sucesos Notables (1665-1703). México, 1946. 3 vols.

Rogers, Woodes. A cruising voyage round the world. London, 1712

Sauer, Carl. Colima of New Spain in the Sixteenth Century. (Ibero-Americana: 29). Berkeley and Los Angeles, 1948.

Schurz, William Lytle. The Manila Galleon. New York, 1939

Shelvocke, George. A voyage round the world, by way of the great South Sea. 2d ed. London, 1757

Sluiter, Engel. "New Light from Spanish Archives on the Voyage of Olivier van Noort: the Vice-Admiral Ship, the Hendrick Frederick, on the West Coast of the Americas (1600)," Bijdragen voor Vaderlandsche Geschiedenis en Oudheidkunde, ser. 7, VIII, ('s-Gravenhage, 1937), 34-48

——. "The word Pechelingue: its derivation and meaning," Hispanic American Historical Review, XXIV (1944), 693-698

[Speilbergen, Joris van]. The East and West Indian Mirror,

being an account of Joris van Speilbergen's voyage round the world (1614-1617), London, Hakluyt Society, 1906

Thomas, Pascoe. A true and impartial journal of a voyage to the South-Sea, and round the globe, in his majesty's ship the Centurion, under the command of commodore George Anson. London, 1745

Torquemada, Juan de. Primera [segunda, tercera] parte de los veinte i vn libros rituales i monarchia indiana. Madrid, 1723. 3 vols.

Vaux, W. S. W., ed. The World Encompassed by Sir Francis Drake. London, Hakluyt Society, 1854

Vázquez de Espinosa, Antonio. Compendio y Descripción de las Indias Occidentales. Washington, 1948

Venegas, Miguel. Noticia de la California y de su conquista. México, 1944. 3 vols.

Villa-Señor y Sanchez, Joseph Antonio de. Theatro Americano, descripcion general de los reynos, y provincias de la Nueva-España, y de sus jurisdicciones. México, 1746-1748. 2 vols.

Wafer, Lionel. A new voyage & description of the isthmus of America. Oxford, Hakluyt Society, 1934

Wagner, Henry Raup. Sir Francis Drake's voyage around the world, its aims and achievements. San Francisco, 1926

———. The Cartography of the Northwest Coast of America to the Year 1800. Berkeley, 1937. 2 vols.

Walter, Richard. A voyage round the world, in the years mdccxl, i, ii, iii, iv. by George Anson, Esq. London, 1748. Note: The abridged Penguin edition has also been used: R. Walter. Lord Anson's Voyage Round the World 1740-1744. West Drayton, 1947

Wycherly, George. Buccaneers of the Pacific. Indianapolis, 1928

Zaragoza, Justo. Piraterías y agresiones de los ingleses, y de otros pueblos de Europa en la América española desde el siglo xvi al xviii deducidas de las obras de D. Dionisio de Alsedo y Herrera. Madrid, 1883

Index

Index

BALBOA, Vasco Nuñez de: 23
Banderas Bay: 49, 90, 218; visited by Swan and Townley,
171-173; Frondat, 209; French traders, 216
Barahona, Jacinto de: 149
Basque pirates: 62
"Batchelor's Delight": 154 ff.
"Begoña": 211, 214-215
Black Anthony: 108
Brouwer, Hendrick: 131
Buccaneers: 14, 135-194, 245
Butler, John: 60 fn.

"CACAFUEGO": 65, 78
Cacao: 31, 34, 47, 84, 199
Caldera, Bay of: 28, 176
Calendar: Gregorian, 18, 81 fn.
California, Lower: 23, 25, 47, 49-52, 103-105, 107, 117, 131-
132, 166-171, 173, 205, 209; visited by Cavendish, 89-94;
Tres Marías pirates, 190, 193-194; Rogers, 212-215; Shel-
vocke, 226; Cochrane, 238
California, Upper: 24, 25, 62, 89; visited by Drake, 74-77
Callao: 65, 104, 126-127, 130, 200
Cañete, Battle of: 112
Caño Island: 27, 65-67, 106, 152, 225
Cardona, Nicolás de: 117
Carvajal, Luis de: 87
Castillo, Antonio del: 87
Cavallos, Agustín de: 106
Cavendish, Thomas: 13, 35, 81-94, 96, 103
Cedros Island: 95, 97, 117
Centeno, Diego: 142
"Centurion": 231 ff.
Chacala Cove: 49, 88, 105
Chamela Bay: 48, 171
Chametla: 51, 173

Dulce Gulf: 27, 152-153, 184
Dutch East India Company: 108
Dutch pirates: 12-13, 101 ff.
Dutch West India Company: 131

EATON, John: 154-157
Elizabeth I: 61-62, 81
Elizabethan pirates: 57-97
"Encarnación": 211, 213-215
England: commercial monopoly in Atlantic, 217
Epidemic disease: 23, 163-165
Esparza: 28, 67, 152, 176-177, 184

FARALLONES: 77
Fernández de Córdoba, Melchor: 113, 116
Flemish pirates: 62, 156 fn.
Fonseca, Gulf of: see Amapala
Food: see victualing
Fortifications: 14; at Acapulco, 42-45, 79, 95, 107, 113-114,
    121-128, 130, 208, 234, 242; at Granada, 178; at Ometepec,
    165; at Panamá, 26, 78, 140, 150, 242; at Pueblo Nuevo,
    151; at Realejo, 29, 67, 156, 175; at Straits of Magellan, 78
French pirates: 12, 62, 110, 124, 135 ff.
Frondat, Nicolas de: 208-209
Funnell, William: 206-207

GALAPAGOS ISLANDS: 156, 163, 200, 210, 217, 221
Gallardillo: 138 fn.
Gálvez, José de: 50
García de Palacio, Diego: 86
Gennes, Jean-Baptiste de: 200
German pirates: 110
"Gloucester": 231 ff.
Gold mines: 11, 27, 30, 46, 146-148, 157, 179, 203
"Golden Hind": 64 ff.